Manage Your Job Search

Johanna Rothman

Manage Your Job Search

Johanna Rothman

This book is for sale at http://leanpub.com/manageyourjobsearch

Published by Practical Ink
www.jrothman.com

Practical **ink**

Cover art: Juli Jorgensen
Book and cover design copyright © 2014 Johanna Rothman.

ISBN-13: 978-0-9854820-7-7

Tweet This Book!

Please help Johanna Rothman by spreading the word about this book on Twitter!

The suggested hashtag for this book is #managejobsearch.

Find out what other people are saying about the book by clicking on this link to search for this hashtag on Twitter:

https://twitter.com/search?q=#managejobsearch

To all the job searchers: I believe in you.
For Mark, Shaina and Naomi, as always.

Contents

Acknowledgments ix

Introduction. xi

PART I
Learn to Manage Your Job Search Project

CHAPTER 1 Become Your Own Project Manager 5

CHAPTER 2 Start Using Your Kanban Board 21

CHAPTER 3 Reflect on the Past Week. 33

CHAPTER 4 Iterate and Organize 45

PART II
Choosing a Career, Interviewing, and Deciding on an Offer

CHAPTER 5 Know Your Previous Job Patterns 53

CHAPTER 6 Write Your Résumé 67

CHAPTER 7 Prepare for the Interview 75

CHAPTER 8 Decide How You Will Decide on an Offer 93

PART III
Build Your Network

CHAPTER 9 Network, Network, Network. 101

CHAPTER 10 Use Social Media to Network 113

PART IV
Iterate Through These Job Hunting Traps and Tips

CHAPTER 11 Avoid These Traps 121

CHAPTER 12 Try These Tips 135

PART V
Special Circumstances:
New Grad, Career Transition, Over 50

CHAPTER 13 What You Need to Know if You Are in Transition . . . 147

CHAPTER 14 Just for People Over 50 153

PART VI
What to Do When Your Job Search Takes Longer than Three Months

CHAPTER 15 It's Been Three Months. Now What? 159

Glossary 165

Annotated Bibliography 167

More from Johanna 173

Acknowledgments

I thank Fred Nothnagel, who runs Wednesday is Networking Day, a networking group for job-seekers in the Boston area, for my first opportunity to speak about this topic. When we spoke in advance of the meeting, he suggested I title my talk "Get Your Next Job the Agile Way."

Well, that started my wheels turning. By the time I'd finished preparing for the talk, I'd outlined this book in my head, and tested it with the 20 or so people at the meeting. They had several "aha" moments.

I thank my reviewers: Holly Bourquin, Shaina Druy, Brian Edlund, Yves Hanoulle, Peter Harris, Bobbi Heath, Lori Howard, Ruth Koch-Ashton, Gerry Kirk, Andy Lester, Ed Schweppe, Dave Smith, Rich Stone, Mike Taylor, James Ward, Serhiy Yevtushenko. I thank Rebecca Airmet, Nancy Groth, and Dave McClintock for their great editing. I thank Jean Jesensky for her indexing and Karen Billipp for her print design. Without their care, you would not be holding this book in print.

Any mistakes are mine.

—Johanna Rothman,
Arlington, Massachusetts

Introduction

You're looking for a job. Maybe you've just graduated from college. Maybe you've been laid off. Or, maybe you've decided that it's time for a career change. Maybe you want a better job. You might even have a better or different reason than the ones I've listed here.

Congratulations!

It's exciting and scary and unpredictable and overwhelming. If you are anything like me, you can be optimistic one moment, pessimistic the next. You can think you have it "all set" and then your stack of company brochures slides off the table onto the floor and you think, "Oh boy, I do *not* have anything together."

And, because it's *all* of those things, and your emotions fly up and down, you just might need some help to find that emotional balance and intellectual focus to stay on track with your job search.

I've hired or consulted on hiring hundreds of people. I've trained thousands of people all over the world about how to hire. I've written two books about hiring. The most recent is *Hiring Geeks That Fit.* Many people think that finding a job is the inverse of hiring. It's not.

Finding a job is dependent on other people. It is an emergent project, where you cannot predict the end date. You create opportunities and take advantage of serendipity.

If you are looking for a job, this book will help you create your system for finding a job. Then, with your system in place, you can iterate on deciding what job to look for, what your résumé should look like, what companies to target, how to interview, and how to get feedback on everything.

This book will help you.
Your job: Find fulfilling work.
My job: Show you a system that works.

PART I
Learn to Manage Your Job Search Project

Do you like looking for a job? Almost no one does. It's overwhelming. You already know you're going to get rejected from jobs that you are qualified for. If *only* you could get in the door . . .

But, managing the rejection in a job hunt is *part* of your job search project. And, sadly, that's the part of the project that most job seekers miss. If you create a project, or a system, you can *manage* your job search, and keep yourself moving, right onto the next potential opportunity. That's what this book is about.

Years ago, when everyone advertised in the Sunday paper, you had just *one* place to look for jobs. Now, there are industry-specific and general online job boards to find and peruse. You need to become a networker extraordinaire, online and in-person. You'll be making decision after decision, each of which will seem to affect your career.

When no one responds to your résumé, it feels like a direct punch to your self-esteem. Don't be surprised: we identify closely with our work. When no one responds to your résumé, you feel personally rejected. When someone asks you for a phone screen or an interview, you feel great! You add these emotional highs and lows to an already intricate, non-linear project with many interruptions and what do you get? A complex project where you can become easily overwhelmed and lose your focus.

How many times have you wished for "magic" in your job hunt? Or, maybe you've "hoped for the best"? Nope, you know that "magic" is not going to happen. And "hope" is not a strategy. How do you maintain your progress and your sanity?

You *can* succeed with an open-ended big project like this. The key is to break your job search into small chunks of work that you can accomplish. You also need to track those chunks of work.

We'll use two project management tools to accomplish this: the "timebox" and the personal kanban board.

A Timebox, p. 165 is when you say, "I'm only going to allow this task to take this much time. Then I'm going to stop, no matter what." You've boxed or limited the time for that work. Timeboxes are useful when the work can take forever and you want to stop for now, and assess where you are.

One-week timeboxes provide a cadence, a rhythm, for your work. That cadence helps you maintain your focus and overcome procrastination. The timebox also forces you to break your work into smaller pieces. That helps you complete specific tasks and feel a sense of accomplishment and progress. That feeling is invaluable in helping you focus, work on your next step, and feel good about your project and yourself—especially when your self-esteem is such a big part of the project.

The personal kanban board helps you determine how much work you can do right now. (Kanban is Japanese for "signboard.") A kanban board is a place where you can see and classify cards in a special way. The personal kanban board helps you see pending and upcoming tasks—especially those that are dependent on something outside your personal control, such as waiting for a response from an email or phone call. It will also provide you with feedback about whether you have over-committed yourself or can take on a bit more. It will help you to not commit to more work than you can actually complete in a single week.

I have noticed that I need both the structure of the big one-week timebox to help me organize my time, and the visualization of the small tasks on the personal kanban board when I work on large open-ended projects, such as a job search. Why? Because as my work moves, visually and physically, across the kanban board, I can see and celebrate what I have finished. That increases my motivation and maintains my focus.

With both the timebox and personal kanban, I have positive feedback. "Oh, I did this. Good for me! I can do this much next week. Ah, I can celebrate my completed work, feel energized and ready for next week. Yay, me!" That is exactly how you should feel at the end of any given week.

By using these techniques, you'll be able to take on small chunks of work and adjust your approach quickly if that approach isn't working.

You may even discover that you like this way of working *so much* that you adopt and adapt it for all of your personal work. I have.

Okay, let's start.

CHAPTER 1
Become Your Own Project Manager

You want to optimize your job search, so you want to spend your time wisely. You know you'll have to repeat the send-a-résumé, wait-for-an-answer loop. You'll have to customize each cover letter for each new opportunity.

What if I told you that you could iterate on everything for your job search project—that you could iterate on how you decide where to look for a job, who to ask for a recommendation, how to network, where to network, absolutely everything for your job search project? And, what if I told you that your data collected from week to week could drive your decision-making?

Once you start networking, sending out resumes, and working your system, you could easily lose track of where you are: Who did you send what to? Who needs a callback? Who needs a customized résumé?

This is why you're using a one-week timebox and personal kanban. You don't plan too much ahead. You plan just enough work that enables you to see all of it. You maintain a rhythm that allows you to reflect.

1.1 Take Advantage of Feedback Opportunities

This is why *you* are your project manager. You don't drown yourself in paper. You keep one week's worth of data at a time, and maybe track some trends about *how* you work. That's it.

When you iterate, you can improve, bit by bit.

1.2 Work on One Action at a Time

One of the problems with iterating is that the realm of possible actions grows exponentially. You can't do everything all in one week. You need to decide how *much* you can accomplish in one week.

You create a rhythm for your work. You see what you can and cannot do in one week. You see your work in progress as you proceed, obtain feedback, and make changes as needed. You will do one small chunk of work at a time and finish it. Then you start something else.

Do *not* try to multitask. That is practically a guarantee your job search will be unsuccessful. Not only will you be less productive, you will make mistakes: call people by the wrong names, send your résumé with the wrong cover letter, sound like an idiot on a phone screen, all kinds of crazy mistakes.

Are you surprised by my insistence against multitasking? Multitasking decreases productivity. Don't believe me? Multitasking takes more time than focusing on one task at a time. It increases the number of errors we make, and it increases our agitation or stress. You can find some of the science here: Multitasking and Task Switching[1], and Multitasking: Switching costs[2].

 Finish one thing. Then another. Take small steps and you will make progress. You'll feel energized as you tackle your job search.

By limiting the *amount* of work in progress, you can actually improve your completion rate, or *throughput*. You will not work on multiple tasks at once—no multitasking. One task at a time!

1.3 Why Finish Small Tasks in Timeboxes?

How will these small tasks inside of timeboxes help you? There is considerable research that confirms we humans like to make progress

---

[1]http://www.umich.edu/~bcalab/multitasking.html
[2]http://www.apa.org/research/action/multitask.aspx

(AMA11). Our motivation and our self-esteem are high when we progress on work that is valuable to us. What could be more valuable than finding a new job?

Along with your accomplishments, you will gain a sense of order, a knowledge that you have your job search under control. You will know that you are working on the most important work at all times. You improve a little bit every week: one, two, or three things. You energize yourself in different arenas, week by week. This will all be helpful when you encounter rejection.

Because you improve your résumé, your networking, your LinkedIn connections, everything about your job search every single week—just a little bit—you improve your ability to show what you have to offer, and potential employers will see your worth.

1.4 What Is Personal Kanban?

Kanban is a Japanese word that means "signboard," p. 165. Kanban is a system of work that originated with Toyota in the 1980s. Taiichi Ohno wrote a book called *The Toyota Production System: Beyond Large-Scale Production* (OHN88) that described how Toyota was able to decrease its inventory and make cars with much less waste.

Kanban is a way of *pulling* work through the system, rather than *pushing* it through the system. Instead of *pushing* all the inventory, or all of the tasks, into production at once, in one big pile, the workers were able to work on a limited set of tasks, *pulling* new work forward as there was space and time.

Personal kanban is a way to schedule work as it flows through the system. When you can see it, you can manage it. This visibility will help you eliminate inefficiencies, offer feedback, and improve your throughput.

Jim Benson and Tonianne Barry wrote the book about personal kanban, *Personal Kanban: Mapping Work | Navigating Life* (BEN11). I suggest you read it if you want to apply it to the rest of your life. It's terrific.

1.5 Why One Week?

Some of you may be familiar with timeboxes, maybe because you've heard of them as a project management approach or via agile approaches. Maybe you're wondering why I insist on one-week timeboxes for your job search.

One week timeboxes help you:

- Maintain your focus
- Allow for faster feedback
- See your progress
- See when you are stuck
- See when you need help from the outside
- See when you are trying to do too much or too little work, and
- See what to measure.

You need to be able to respond quickly to changes in the job search environment. Do you need to update your résumé? Take advantage of a new job fair? Network in a new way, at a new location, or with a new group? When you work in a one-week timebox with a visual representation of your search, and then look for feedback, you can see what to keep and what to change.

 When you are your own project manager, you can see what's working and what's not working. Experiment and toss what's not working. Keep what is working.

1.6 Manage Your Risk

As a job hunter, you want to manage the risk of not finding the perfect job in a reasonable timeframe. How do you manage risk? By making your deliverables small and staying focused.

The bigger the chunk, the harder your job hunt is, and the less motivated you are. That's why you're going to use a one-week timebox—to keep your motivation high and to help you visualize your next steps.

1.7 Make Sure You Can See Your Work

Your first task is to organize yourself to accomplish anything. This will help you take control of your job search. Creating, visualizing, organizing, and ranking your tasks, which I like to call ToDos, is key to accomplishing your goal: getting your next job.

Why Am I Calling Tasks ToDos?

You might call your tasks "Actions" or "Tasks." I call them "ToDos."

I call them that because they might not be well-formed when I put them on my list. I want to make sure that if I think of it, I write it on my list. If these ideas are not actionable, my first action might be to make the ToDo actionable. The next time, I'll use this feedback and create a better ToDo. But I want that ToDo on my list.

As you become better at your job search and at using personal kanban, maybe all of your ToDos will become actionable. *Terrific.* In the meantime, if you think about a ToDo, write it down. Don't worry about what it is. Write it down, and then decide how to deal with it.

First, you'll create a workspace that will allow you to visualize your work. You have to *physically* see your work to make this approach work for you. Even if you only have part-time use of a desk, you can make this approach work.

You will be creating your personal kanban board that looks like this.

Ready To Do	In Progress	The Pen	Done

To create your workspace, you'll first need to claim some blank wall, ideally near your phone, computer, and desk. You will need a space large enough to see your work. Think in terms of 3 feet high by 2 feet wide. Here are some possibilities for you, aside from wall space:

- A whiteboard
- A piece of flipchart paper
- The front of a refrigerator
- A notebook
- A corkboard
- A noteboard[3]

If you use a notebook, use a large one that will lie flat when you open it up, so that you use two facing sheets, as in this picture.

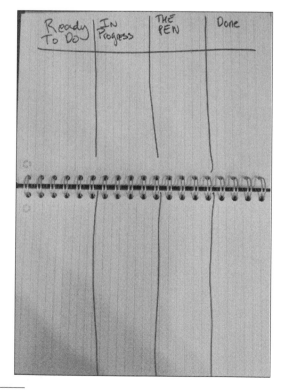

---

[3]noteboard.com

If you use a noteboard from noteboard[4], here's what it might look like when you start:

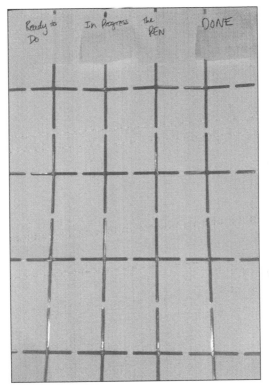

Your columns don't need to align, regardless of the board you use. The noteboard is a little too wide for four columns. Maybe if you used slightly wider stickies than I did, the columns would line up nicely. I like the length in the columns, because I have many little ToDos. I want the space for them. I don't care if they line up perfectly.

Whatever you do, make sure you have a big visible board. That way you can see your status at a moment's glance. You don't have to work to see the status; you see it immediately.

---

[4]noteboard.com

Your board works because you can see your status—your work and your progress—at one time. If you can't see it all, your board is not going to work for you. Experiment with another kind of board.

There are only four columns on your board. The "Ready To Do" column will have all of your ToDos for one week. The "In Progress" column will have all of your work that you have started during that week. And the "Done" column will have all of the work that you completed during the week. "The Pen" column is a special column for the work you can't complete because you depend on other people to finish that work, i.e., call-backs or email responses. Think of "The Pen" as a corral, where you track those up-in-the-air, not-quite-done pieces of work that you can't finish alone.

1.8 Create Your ToDos

Now, you have your board or your notebook. It's time to transfer your ToDo list to your board or notebook.

Your first step is to write everything on your ToDo list onto stickies, one to a sticky. If you use cards, assume cards when I say stickies, okay?

1.9 What Might You Do First?

Here's how I would start in Week One. You might not like these ToDos in this order. That's okay. Use this list as a guide, and change it. Consider this list a template for your first week.

1. Create a barebones LinkedIn profile with your name, email, education, and most recent work experience. If you are a new grad, where you graduated and your graduation date.
2. Create a draft résumé.
3. Ask three people to review your résumé and email it to them.
4. Decide who your references will be, and ask them to be your references.

5. Make a list of where to network in-person this month.
6. Start sending connection requests to people you know on LinkedIn.
7. Update your profile on LinkedIn. Now is the time to start crafting your profile, adding value to each line on the profile. You might decide to do some of this before sending connection requests.
8. Endorse people on LinkedIn, so you give before you get. (Note: as of this writing, endorsements are becoming less useful, so you may decide this is not worth your while.)
9. Take your LinkedIn photo, p. 24 and post it, if you have not done so before now. People with photos on LinkedIn are seven times more likely to hear from a hiring manager.
10. Start looking at online job boards, now that you have a reasonable résumé and a reasonable LinkedIn profile. (If your résumé and your profile are ready earlier, you can move this up the list.)
11. Start networking in person, by participating, not just attending, some of those networking events you considered in #5.
12. Research specific company #1 that you would like to work for, assuming you know what it is.
13. Research specific company #2 that you would like to work for, assuming you know what it is.

In addition, if you are senior enough and there is enough demand in your field, you may want to contact a recruiter. For example, in my field, software, once you have several years of experience, many of the jobs are not advertised. You need to know somebody or know a recruiter. This is why you want to Network With People Who are Loose Connections, p. 116, and why your network is so critical to your success.

What might you do in Week Two? Update your résumé, continue networking in person, continue networking on LinkedIn, consider other job boards. You want to reflect on what you did and did not accomplish in Week One, and how you felt about your progress before you decide where to go with Week Two. Maybe, you prefer to call everyone you know, instead of focusing your efforts on your online profile. Make conscious choices.

Why Focus So Much on LinkedIn for the First Week?

As you've noticed by now, LinkedIn is a huge part of making connections and becoming known in your job search. I have focused a significant part of your first week's ToDos on LinkedIn. Why?

LinkedIn is, right now, the 600-pound gorilla. If you want people to know you professionally, you *must* be on LinkedIn. If you don't exist on LinkedIn, you don't exist. You might not like it, but it's the current truth

You don't have to use LinkedIn to heavily network, although I do recommend you consider it. But, if you don't have a profile, with a picture, potential employers will not find you. It's that simple.

You, as the candidate, want every tool at your disposal. LinkedIn is one of your primary tools. Use it.

Week One is about getting ready to put your best self on the market. Week Two is what you do with that first feedback. Maybe potential employers don't understand your résumé. Okay, you'll update it until they do. Or, you'll spend a little money on a résumé-writing service. Maybe you don't have references yet. You need them. Keep asking. Maybe you don't have any ideas about where to network. Keep looking.

If you don't like my possible Week One and Week Two ToDos, that's fine. As long as you are taking steps, you'll be fine. Just Don't Leave a Zombie Profile on LinkedIn, p. 131 when a potential employer looks for you. *That's bad.* No one wants to hire a zombie.

1.10 Keep ToDos Small and Independent

Keep two things in mind as you create your ToDos. You will make more progress with your job search if you keep your ToDos small and independent.

Some of your ToDos will have natural dependencies. There's a natural dependency between writing the résumé and the résumé review. That's fine.

But sometimes multiple dependent ToDos can masquerade as a single large ToDo. I recently met someone who had a whole series of ToDos centered around a job fair: research the companies, decide whether to participate in the job fair, compose introductions, maybe even more ToDos. You can decouple these preparatory ToDos from each other.

Here's how I would do it. First, do some research to see whether this job fair is for you. Now, this might mean a longer research ToDo, or even several research ToDos that target specific companies or opportunities for the job fair.

Are you flexible about the type of job you are looking for? Based on your job research, you might compose different introductions, emphasizing different aspects of your experience, for different potential employers.

Your job fair ToDos now look like this:

Decision: Attend this job fair: yes/no? (This decision is the triggering decision for all the other ToDos)

Each of these ToDos is now independent:

- Research Company X (timebox to 15 minutes)
- Research Company Y (timebox to 15 minutes)
- Research Company Z (timebox to 15 minutes)
- Network with David C. about Company X. Didn't he work there?
- Work on Intro 1 for Position A
- Work on Intro 2 for Position B
- Print 25 résumés before Tuesday

1.11 **Rank Your ToDos**

Depending on your field and your experience, your ToDos will be specific to you. However, for many people, First Week ToDos will look similar.

As an example, let's say you need to: research a company, review a specific job board for open positions, and call your old boss for a reference—you would have three stickies. That looks like this:

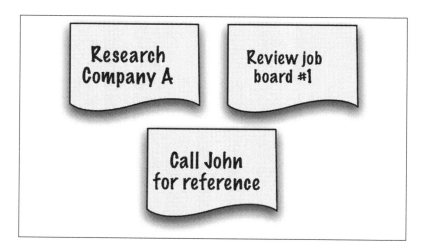

Now, for simplicity's sake, let's rank these three stickies. They are all important. In fact, you could say they are all the #1 priority. But they can't be. You need to decide which one to do first.

Here is where the fact that you have your ToDos on something moveable is helpful. Take all the stickies. Line them up in some order, even if you think that order is wrong, on the wall or on your desk. Now, step back so you can get a little perspective.

Maybe you made "Call John for reference" #1. Is that okay? If so, leave it there. Maybe you made "Research Company A" #2. Is that okay? If not, exchange the sticky underneath it with that one.

Keep sorting until you are happy with the sort order. Remember, you can only have one #1 ranked item. You can only have one #2. You are only one person, so you can only do one thing at a time—that's why you can only have one #1.

What if you can't decide between two stickies? You really have two critical stickies, and you want to accomplish both of them this week. What do you do then? You have some options:

- Do the smallest one first. Sometimes, accomplishing *something* is better than fretting about the priority.
- Toss a coin. If they are the same priority, who cares which one you do first?
- Break the ToDos apart, and see if they have ToDos underneath, one of which might be more critical than another.

1.12 Limit Your Week's Work

At some point, you realize you have too many items for one week. Review all of your ToDos. Now, think about your week and how much time you can devote to your job search. Are you still working a day job and only looking for a job part time? Are you devoting all of your energy to finding a job? You will be able to accomplish different numbers of ToDos based upon your available time.

Make your ToDos small enough to complete within an hour or two. That's how you make your job search successful—and more flexible.

Just as I suggested about what to do with the job fair ToDo, you can learn to break your work up into small chunks. Here are some tips:

1. If you are not sure how long any of your work will take, consider using one-hour and two-hour timeboxes for all of your ToDos. Many of us humans stink at estimation. We tend to be either optimistic or pessimistic. Rarely are we accurate.

2. What is the first thing you have to accomplish for your next ToDo? Do that. Is there more to do for that ToDo? Now, write everything else down on separate stickies. You have something larger than you thought. *That's okay.* Remember that for next week's planning.

3. Some people think if they take their total time per day for their job search, and divide that by the total number of one hour timeboxes, they can use that amount of time for the number of ToDos. If you find that helpful, let me know.

As you practice your ToDo planning, you will become better at it.

The most useful information I know: Write everything down on a sticky. Rank the stickies. Start at the top, and keep working your way down.

 Do not try to do *everything* you can think of for your job search in the first week. You will make yourself nuts. Think of the first week as laying the foundation for a successful job search.

What if you *know* you have too much to do for your first week? Create a Parking Lot for Work You Don't Want to Lose, p. 18. For now, place all the stickies you can't accomplish on the Parking Lot. You'll assess it next week, when you can see whether that work is still useful. For now, you don't have to consider it. You've written it down. You don't have to worry about it.

1.13 Use a Parking Lot for Work You Don't Want to Lose

You have work you don't want to forget about, and you don't want to do it right now. Use a parking lot to hold a sticky so you can postpone dealing with it *right now*. I keep the Parking Lot separate from my Personal Board, which is why you don't see it in the pictures. You can keep it on your board, but then you might feel stressed by all that potential work. I don't recommend it.

I keep it separate, because I don't want to think about it until it's time to plan for the next week.

 "Perfection is the enemy of the good." —Gustave Flaubert. If you wait for everything to be perfect, you could wait a

long time. Do not wait for a perfect picture or a perfect
résumé or a perfect profile. You have to progress on this
task, mark it done, and move to the next one. If you are
confused by good enough and perfection, see Perfection
Rules Trap Us Every Time, p. 121.

Remember when you ranked the work? If you are stuck on work
that does not add value to your overall job search, you will *not* make
progress. That's another reason for one-week timeboxes. You have an
opportunity every week to look back and reflect on your progress. You
have the chance to see whether where you invested your energy was
the right place. And, you only spent a week doing so!

1.14 But I Like to Use Electronic Tools

I bet some of you are thinking, "Johanna can't fool me. I know *just* the
right tool for this: a spreadsheet, or a kanban tool."

You are correct. This is personal kanban. If electronic tools tempt
you for the first four weeks of this approach:

DO NOT BE TEMPTED BY THE DARK SIDE.

I am serious.

When you use tangible physical objects, such as stickies or cards,
you will make better decisions about your tasks. There is something
about the tactile nature of the cards or stickies that will provide you
with better feedback about your ToDos. Not just the size of the ToDos,
but better decisions about how you rank them.

I see this with my clients when they have to make project
portfolio decisions. If they can do this for a month while they are
learning to manage their project portfolios with millions of dollars at
stake, I bet you can do this for a month while you learn to manage
your job search.

Trust me for four weeks. After that, you can decide what to do.
Really.

1.15 **Now Do This**

1. Create your board. Make sure you have enough space on your board.

2. Create your first set of ToDos. Write them all out. Don't worry if you have too many. Make sure they are independent. You don't know how many you can do in a week yet. If you have too many for a week, you will learn how many you can and cannot do.

3. Rank your ToDos.

CHAPTER 2
Start Using Your Kanban Board

By now, you have a board, with a ranked list of ToDos. You've ranked your week's list of work. Now, let's start making this project management approach work for your job search.

2.1 Start Your Week on a Wednesday

I suggest you start your week on a Wednesday. There is a great reason to *not* start your week on a Monday. We are human. We don't always complete everything we think we can when we create a plan. If we have not been diligent about completing our ToDos, we tend to want to "make up" the time over the weekend. We think this allows us to catch up in time for Monday. I don't want you to do that.

If you start your week on Wednesday, you'll work at a sustainable pace, and take time for yourself. You are *not* just your job search.

What if you're unemployed and your local Department of Employment Security wants to know about your job search data? I bet you are smart enough to know how to track that data with a spreadsheet for them, either Wednesday to Wednesday, or Monday through Friday, if that's what's required.

But really, who's in charge of your job search? You or the Department of Employment Security?

2.2 Plan Your First Week

Remember when I asked you to make each of your ToDos small, so you could accomplish each of them in a couple of hours or less? That was so you could do *something*, and then get feedback on it. If that something is your résumé, great. If that something is some networking, excellent. If that something is asking for references or recommendations, terrific. Maybe that something is to get on LinkedIn.

LinkedIn is an excellent place to start your job hunt. It's a large complex task in and of itself (Where do I start? What do I do? How do I use this?). Furthermore, the first hurdle of job searching is networking. You have to be found if you want to find a job.

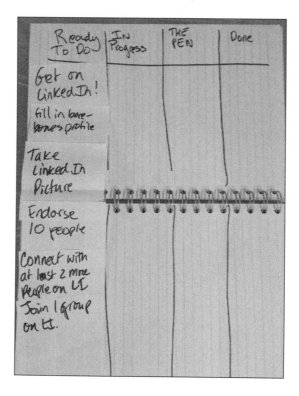

Let's walk through the example of this board as your first week. Your first sticky is to "Get on LinkedIn!" You move that sticky to "In Progress".

Now, you go to http://www.linkedin.com and sign up for an account. You're done. You move the sticky to "Done". Easy.

2.3 Work in Sequence

You may be tempted to add a few connections when you sign up for your LinkedIn account. What could it hurt? You think, "While I'm here, I can do more."

You have some choices. You can make a sticky, "Add a few connections" and put it on the top of the list and move it to "In Progress." Remember, you want to see all of the work you are doing. Or, you can make that sticky and move it to the bottom of the "Ready To Do" list because you haven't thought about the relative rank of "Add a few connections" to your overall list. That's what I would do.

Do not assume "Add a few connections" should automatically be the next ToDo on your list. Just because it's easy does not make it the next priority. In fact, I suggest you should *not* ask people to connect with you until you have a bare-bones profile, which is your next sticky. Why? Because you look like a zombie and no one wants to connect with a zombie, p. 131.

But it's more than the zombie problem. You want to be intentional with your ToDo list. Just because something is easy, and appears to be something you can do quickly, is *not* a reason to put it on the top of your list. You've already decided on the order of the work. You want to be intentional if you decide to change the order of the work.

You can change your mind. Don't create more work for yourself unless you intentionally choose to do so. Do the work in rank order of importance to your job search. Make more stickies instead, and add them to the bottom of your list, or the Parking Lot.

Take the next sticky, "Fill in bare-bones profile." Move the sticky to "In Progress".

If you've been working for more than a few years or for more than one or two organizations, you might think you have to remember everything you've done and the value you've added to the organization. But remember, this sticky says "bare-bones profile." That means you add the dates and names of every place you've worked. That's it. That allows you to complete this sticky in less than a couple of hours, no matter how long you've been working. Once you're done, you move that Sticky to "Done".

2.3.1 *Post a Picture on LinkedIn*

If you are looking for a job, you need a photo on LinkedIn. According to LinkedIn's senior manager of corporate communications, Krista Canfield, "Folks who have a photo are seven times more likely to have their profile viewed in general than folks who don't have a photo." (SAL11).

As of this writing, LinkedIn is the essential place for online business networking. If you are not on LinkedIn, you don't exist for the purposes of finding a job. Create a profile on LinkedIn and post a good-enough picture.

You have to be *found* to get over the first hurdle of networking. Take the darn picture and post it already. Remember, the growth mindset is not about perfection; it's about doing something reasonable and getting some feedback. Take a picture of your smiling face, please. Make sure we can tell who *you* are; your picture should be a head shot of you—not your dog, not your child, not your hockey team, and definitely not anything below your waist.

Why am I so vehement about a headshot, and nothing below your waist? I've seen many pictures of people on LinkedIn. One gentleman is a member of Red Sox nation. If you're not from the Boston area, that is a geographic area that runs from roughly Maine to Connecticut, but can exist anywhere a transplanted Red Sox fan has moved. He wanted a job with a sports management firm. He had dressed in all of his Red Sox paraphernalia: including the socks. He was not attractive.

His excitement about the Red Sox might help him get a job with a sports management firm. But the socks? Not so much.

Ladies, no glamour shots. Everyone, no sports shots, and a smiling face, please. This is business. Please post an image that you wouldn't mind seeing at work. It can be informal, but it needs to be work-appropriate.

Upload the photo to LinkedIn and move that Sticky to "Done". Now take a moment to celebrate. You've accomplished a very important step in your job search.

This is how you move down your "Ready To Do" list. Do the minimum to *complete* the sticky. Do not do any more than that.

Some of your stickies are going to take longer than these examples. Maybe you're going to use your built-in camera on your computer for your picture, and it takes you the better part of an hour to take a picture. Maybe you want to use the camera on your smartphone, and it still takes you more than an hour. That's okay. The idea is that you keep making progress on your "Ready To Do" list. And, that you don't have more than one item in your "In Progress" list. Your goal is still to keep every task to one hour.

Remember that you want to do the minimum to complete the sticky. No gilding the lily here. Do what you need to do, and be done with it. You have a job to find.

2.4 What Does Your Board Look Like?

The image on page 26 shows what your week looks like as you work partway through it:

You've moved three tasks from "Ready to Do" to "In Progress" to "Done". You've accomplished half of the ToDos on your list! Doesn't that feel fantastic? Congratulate yourself!

 The smaller your ToDos, the faster you move work across the board. The more you retain your focus. The less multitasking you do.

The board makes all your work visible. You can see the flow and rhythm of your work through these categories. When each of your tasks takes less than two hours, you are more likely to finish them. You know when the work is complete. You retain focus.

When I Made My ToDos Smaller, I Succeeded Faster

"I used this approach. When I made my ToDos smaller, I was more successful. When I didn't, I was less successful.

Why was I inconsistent? Because I was inconsistent with my networking. I didn't want to see the feedback from my board. So I didn't look. I had the data. I just didn't want to look.

My advice? Use small ToDos and look at your data. It took me almost a year to find a job. If I'd looked at my data, maybe it would have taken me less time." —An over-50 job hunter

Looking for a job is difficult work. You will be interrupted by phone calls or emails or notifications from LinkedIn. The board allows you to literally see where you are, recover from the context switch, and return to work. You know exactly where you were and what you were doing.

2.5 Should I Use Stickies or Cards?

You can use cards instead of stickies on your board. If you have a corkboard, you might prefer index cards.

I like stickies because they are easy to move. If you like, you can use one color for résumé-related work, one color for networking, one color for meetings, etc. I would get confused. I use yellow stickies, because I like yellow.

Another option: Use cards and buy gluesticks that are the same adhesive as stickies. Now you have something more tangible than a sticky, and it's not as flimsy.

Make sure you use something that provides you tactile feedback.

2.6 How to Use "The Pen" Column

Look back at the picture of your board in progress. See that third column? The one labeled "The Pen"? You've probably noticed that I haven't talked about it yet.

"The Pen" is a place where you can keep wayward tasks, dependent tasks that need to be done later, or tasks that you've started but can't mark as done because they are out of your control. Usually this involves waiting on others for something: a callback, a return email, something.

Say you make a phone call and do not reach the person. You have at least these choices:

- You can mark the call as "Done", create a new sticky that says you need to call back or email the contact, and put the new sticky on the bottom of your "Ready To Do" column

- You can make a note on the sticky, of the time you called, and put the sticky back on the "Ready To Do" column
- You can make a note on the sticky, of the time you called, and put the sticky in "The Pen" column

When you put the note on the sticky, you have a note of the dates and times you attempted to contact this person. You can decide if it's worth calling this person yet again, or if this person is a dead end and you should call someone else instead. Or, whether you should use a different approach to contact him/her. You have the data at your fingertips, literally.

Notice, that you can't call the task done, because it's not. Whatever you do, do not leave the task "In Progress" because it's not.

"The Pen" allows you to corral all those not-quite-done tasks that you have no control over, usually you are waiting for others for something: a callback, a return email, something.

Make sure if you move a task into "The Pen" that you note what you are waiting for, or the state you left the ToDo in. For example, if you asked Stephanie, your old boss, for a reference, and you want to confirm that she will provide one, your ToDo was "Ask Stephanie for reference."

Move that sticky from "In Progress" into "The Pen" column. Write on the sticky, "Called Jan 4, 2:37pm, left vmail. Said would check with her via email in two days if I hadn't heard back."

Now, you need to also make yourself a ToDo sticky: Write an email to Stephanie in two days if I don't hear from her before then.

2.7 Why Limit The Pen?

Watch that "The Pen" column doesn't get too large. Everything in "The Pen" is work in progress. If it's in "The Pen", you're not limiting your work in progress. If you are asking too much of other people, they will not respond to your requests for help. How large is too large? I don't know. For now, try a limit of three open items in your Pen. If you need to enlarge your Pen, ask yourself why. If you have a good reason, fine. Be honest with yourself.

The reason I'm suggesting you limit the items in your Pen is this: Are those people going to call you back? In a job search, you can waste tons of time on dead end "leads"—leads that are not real leads. If people are not going to call you back or email you back, acknowledge that and move on. Do not spend one more second on those people and transition your search or networking time to people who do appreciate what you have to offer.

When you spend time calling back and calling back and calling back and calling back, your self-esteem plummets. "The Pen" shows you the data about the number of times you have called or emailed. Use that data to decide how often to keep calling or emailing.

Another reason to limit "The Pen" to three items is to make sure you are not trying to contact people outside of their regular working hours. It's too easy for some of us to become afraid or shy and say, "I'd rather not face the potential rejection. I'll call when I think Sheila won't be at her desk." Sometimes this thought isn't even conscious, but it's still there.

Hey! This is *your* job search. You can be afraid. You can be shy. But this is *your* job search. No one is going to search for you. Here's what I think to myself when I call or email a client and check in. I would rather know earlier that the client wants or doesn't want me. If I know earlier that they want me, wonderful! I have an engagement. If I know the client doesn't want me, I have the option of asking why, and I continue down my list. I don't have to wonder. I don't have to spend any more emotional time on that client. I am done. I am free to pursue the next potential client on my list.

The more emotional time you spend hoping that the potential employers you have in your Pen will love you, the less free you are to pursue other potential employers. That can make you nuts. Don't make yourself nuts. You might need "The Pen" to be more than three items, but don't let "The Pen" get too large. Reflect on the size of "The Pen" in your retrospective.

If you don't have any more potential employers on your list, write a sticky that says "Find more leads" or something like that. You will have to break that sticky down into other tasks, such as "Search LinkedIn groups" or "Search Monster" or "Search Dice" or "Network more in-person" or "Generate a target list of companies" or "Get feedback on résumé" or something. But, if you leave "The Pen" large, you are not doing yourself any favors. This is why you do retrospectives and collect data. To be honest with yourself.

2.8 Try This For a Week and See What Happens

If you kept your ToDo stickies small, you probably got a ton of work done. If you discover your ToDos were too large, you probably had more trouble. And, if you encountered some rejection, you may not have accomplished much of anything. That happens sometimes.

If you did not do the work, admit it. If you admit it, you can see what traps you encounter. I have some suggestions for how to manage the traps in Avoid These Traps, p. 133.

2.9 Review Your Emergent Project

Because you are dependent on someone else—your eventual hiring manager—for the end of this project, you can't predict the end of this project. That makes this an emergent project. You need to adapt to the current situation. You need to be prepared for whatever comes.

Emergent projects are not the same as any other project. You want to take advantage of opportunities and replan when an opportunity presents itself. You will definitely change your priorities week by week. If you make sure to keep your ToDos small enough, and then complete them, you can adjust your priorities even more quickly than that.

That's why I want you to have a visual board, not an electronic board. That's why I want you to limit your ToDos to two hours or less. That's why I want you to ask for feedback throughout your job search.

That's why I want you to limit your work in progress, and limit the number of items in "The Pen".

Step back for a minute and look at your job search as a big picture. Some of you might think of this as "going meta."

We are using some agile and lean project management principles in this project:

- Increased information flow with short feedback loops. You get this with the one-week timebox, measuring progress, adapting to feedback, and using your board.
- Avoiding procrastination and defeatism by limiting work in progress. You get this by only performing one ToDo at a time, and by performing your work in sequence.
- You replan every week, so you can use the information as you garner it. If you discover a great new place for networking, in person or online, great. You can take advantage of it. You are not stuck doing something that is not going to help you.
- Agile and lean principles work for regular projects. They are ideal for emergent projects, where you cannot predict the result.

2.10 Now Do This

1. Did you take a picture and post it on your LinkedIn page? If not, do it now. You can use your smartphone, a friend's smartphone, or your computer's camera. Take the picture and post it. That picture is good enough for now. Remember, people with a photo are much more likely to be viewed on LinkedIn. You can't get a job if no one is looking at you. Now move that sticky into the "Done" column.

2. If your tasks are too big, take your top ranked task and break it into smaller tasks. Now, do the first task in its entirety. You not only feel great but you have data so you can calibrate the rest of your work.

3. If you have perfection rules about accomplishing work, address them now. Don't let the perfect get in the way of the "good enough," especially when it comes to making progress on the rest of the work you need to do for your job search.

CHAPTER 3
Reflect on the Past Week

You've had a little practice moving tasks across the board.

In projects, we want to reflect after we've had a chance to do some work. Now it's time to measure data, collect feedback, and reflect. Because a job search is an emergent project, you'll be generating many of your own activities. You want feedback from yourself to see what you've accomplished and how you feel about what you've done and not done.

You've tried your one week timebox. You've created your chart, written your ToDos, and ranked them. You've limited your week's worth of work, made the chunks of work small enough to finish, and made sure your ToDos were independent. You've used your Big and Visible Board to track the progress of your ToDos as you worked on them during the week. Now is the time to obtain both quantitative and qualitative feedback.

Remember, the growth mindset is about doing something, getting a little feedback, and seeing what is working for you.

3.1 Measure What You Accomplished Quantitatively

An important piece of feedback is charting how many of your tasks you actually accomplished during the week and when you accomplished them. You can see how many tasks you completed. If you wanted, you could graph this.

You can use a chart similar to this one as a start at looking at how many tasks you complete during a week and over time. You use this data to plan for the future, assuming ensuing weeks are similar.

	Wednesday	Thursday	Friday	Saturday	Sunday	Monday	Tuesday	
Daily total	3	4	3	0	2	3	4	
Cumulative weekly total	3	7	10	10	12	15	19	19

Week

1	2	3	4	5	6	7	8	9	10	...
19										

On the top, you look at the number of tasks you complete each day. At the same time each day—pick a time you know you will keep—count the number of tasks you completed. You should have some days with zero in them. You are supposed to take some days off. I don't know which days those are though, which is why there are seven days up there.

On the bottom, you track the weeks of your job search. Since all the tasks are supposed to be relatively small, you want to just count the number of ToDos. No, the tasks are not *normalized*, so those analytical types who are saying, "JR, what are you thinking? Some of these are longer and some are shorter?" They are. It's okay. Make all your tasks shorter and they will be closer to normalized.

See how many tasks you finished in your week. Did you accomplish all the tasks in your "Ready To Do" column? Did you have extra time? Did you struggle to accomplish everything? You can use this feedback to gauge the amount of work you are able to do in one week and predict the work for the next week.

Do not beat yourself up about any number at all, unless that number is zero. If that number is zero, have a discussion with yourself about why. Use the Facilitated Conversation technique, p. 51 if you want to. Try to Do Something Every Day, p. 155.

You can also use this chart to see how many tasks were left over at the end of the week. What is left in your "In Progress" column? If there is anything there at the end of the week, only you know why. Your ToDos may be too large. You might have overestimated how much you can accomplish in one week. You might be multitasking between tasks, not finishing any of them. Maybe you have other responsibilities that take time away from your job search. Identifying these stumbling blocks is one of the reasons that it's important to reflect over just one week: you have a chance of remembering what happened.

You use this data to predict what you can do for next week. You're not trying to *increase* what you can do. You're trying to *plan* what you can do, so you can make steady progress. That way, if a prospective employer asks you to mail a résumé, you know what will have to come off the list.

3.2 Measure Your Job Search Progress

Lori Howard, a job search coach, suggests these measurements:

1. Number of job leads found.
2. Number of people contacted. You might want to separate this for your different networking approaches: LinkedIn, Twitter, and in person. Although, if you're doing it right, you might not be able to tell.
3. Number of job applications submitted.
4. Number of phone interviews.

5. Number of in-person interviews.

6. Number of offers.

If you don't have any job leads, maybe it's because you're not networking. If you're not networking, maybe it's because you don't have any job leads? Those two are linked, and you need both networking and job leads to generate more of each.

You need to apply for jobs in order to get the phone screens. Once you have a phone interview, now you can see if you can get the in-person interview. You have to ace the in-person interview, and you'll be competing with other job seekers for that job. You can't convert every interview to an offer. But you can track how many offers you do receive.

If you start tracking your data, you can see where you go awry.

3.3 Ask for Some Qualitative Feedback

As you work through the week, ask for feedback as you finish your tasks. Ask your family, friends, colleagues, fellow networkers. Are you finishing your work faster? Are you responding faster to their requests? Are you accomplishing what you wanted to accomplish? Are you happier or more content with your job search?

You might not feel happy during a job search. People often feel that it's a time of chaos because of all the change and uncertainty. Happiness may not be an emotion you feel during chaos. However, if you feel as if you are making progress, you may not feel quite as much discomfort, even if you don't feel happy.

3.3.1 *Review Your Qualitative Data*

Your chart provided you with quantitative data. You can ask for qualitative feedback from your family, friends, and colleagues. Now it's time to reflect on your first week in a formal way, to see what you have accomplished, and to see if you want to do anything differently for the next week.

Think of your project as "try something small; learn rapidly; use that to plan next." You have a chance to change your approach immediately if it's not working.

After each week you'll want to reflect on the previous week. Qualitative data is just as important, if not more so, than quantitative data. Here are several ways to reflect on your previous week's activities.

3.4 Try Plus/Minus/Change

Take a fresh sheet of regular paper. Draw two lines down, dividing it into three roughly even parts. Label the first third "Plus", the next third "Minus", and the last third "Change". If you're anything like me, you'll use symbols to represent the columns. The triangle symbol is the Greek symbol for "Delta," the change symbol.

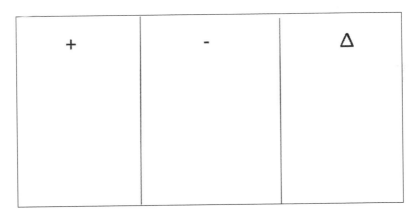

Now, take a look at your board or notebook—what you accomplished or did not accomplish—for your first week. This activity is not about beating yourself up. This activity is about collecting information. So, take a deep breath, and be honest with yourself.

What makes you feel good about the past week? Note that in the plus column. What is not so hot about the past week? Note that in the minus column. What would you like to change about the next week? Put that in the change column.

This activity is about looking at what you were able to accomplish as opposed to the actual outcome of what you did. Sometimes in a job search, it matters more that you have four phone screens, rather than that you did a great job on them. You don't always have control over the kind of job you do on the phone screen. You do have a little more control about *getting* the phone screen. So, it's more of a plus to get the phone screen.

 Sometimes activity is the right thing to do. Especially if you're experimenting in your job search. If you don't think your experiments are helping, that's also feedback. Try Proud/Oops to learn more about your experiments.

Now you have data with which to plan your next week of work for your job search. As you plan your ToDos and chunks of work, keep your pluses, minuses, and changes in mind. You may have made commitments already that you have to honor. Fine. Honor them. And, as you continue your job search, you can experiment with ideas and see whether they lead to more pluses or more minuses. You can't tell until you try.

You will need to *experiment* in your job search. You won't know if a job fair is a good idea, or if a phone screen with a particular company is a good idea, or if some other approach is a good idea until you try it. When you experiment, and find a way to get some feedback, you learn something.

Now, if you just did +/-/Δ all the time, you would get bored and stop doing retrospectives. So, here are some other options for your retrospectives:

3.5 Consider Proud/Oops

In retrospective literature, this is called "Proud/Sorry". I prefer "Proud/Oops", because I feel as if I've made an "oops," when I've made a mistake such as the ones you are likely to encounter.

I bet that during the week you had moments when you felt proud of what you had accomplished. And, you may have had moments when you felt like you blew it. This works best when you write these moments down, so you can revel in your accomplishments and forgive yourself for not performing up to your high standards.

Take two pieces of paper. Label one "Proud". Label the other "Oops".

Now, use your stickies for recording every event you can remember for the past week, where you felt pride or sorrow. If you had no real feeling about any event, you can skip it. These stickies may be different than your ToDos. If some of your ToDos were the events, feel free to take your ToDo stickies and use them.

If you discover that you have all "Oops" events, do not allow yourself to use this activity anymore. Why? Because if you insist on thinking everything you do is wrong, you are not being fair to yourself. Look back at your board. I bet there are a number of stickies in your "Done" column. I bet you were not a total jerk with everyone you interacted with. I bet you did not insult people. If you cannot remember all the great things you accomplished, be it ever so small, do not use this approach as a retrospective.

This is supposed to be an honest look back at your week. If you are not going to use it that way, either don't do it alone or don't use it. If you need a partner for this, try a facilitated conversation in addition to or instead of "Proud/Oops".

3.6 Have a Facilitated Conversation

In a facilitated conversation (STA00), you have a conversation with someone who prompts you with these questions. If necessary, you have the conversation with yourself. It's better to have a conversation with another person. You ask four questions of this form, giving yourself enough time to answer each question fully before continuing to the next one:

- What data did you notice about the week, what stood out for you?

- What were your emotional reactions to the week? What made you happy? Where were you challenged? Where were you frustrated?
- What were your insights? What did you learn?
- What one or two things will you do based on this week?

This is great to do if you are an extrovert, and like to "talk things out," rather than "think things through." I'm a talker by nature, so I can think first but talking sometimes allows me to work a problem out better and faster. If you are a thinker by nature, spend time with each question, and journal your answers, thinking and writing.

Spend as much time as you need. This activity is not a race. And you talkers—there is no trophy for speeding through the answers.

If you need other options for your retrospectives, I highly recommend Derby and Larsen's *Agile Retrospectives: Making Good Teams Great* (DER06). You are not part of a team, but you can use ideas from the book.

3.7 Gather Your Big Picture

Sometimes, you need to start with the big picture before you can gather any data (WEI13). There might not be anything *wrong*, but you might need to journal about your week. If you are that kind of a person, start with these questions:

- How did I happen to get here? (Write about how you feel about the past.)
- How do I feel about being here? (Write about how you feel about the present.)
- What would I like to have happen? (Write about your hopes for the future.)

These questions start with the past, bring you through to the present, and help you imagine the future.

When you start with the first question, "How did I happen to get here?" you might start with the networking you made this past week.

If it's early in your job search, maybe you want to journal about why you started to look for a job. Especially if you are the kind of person who thinks things through, journaling may be just the thing to help you see what's going on for you.

Now, move to the second question, "How do I feel about being here?" Write about this past week, and your emotions about today, as you reflect. Are you going through the motions? Are you engaged? If not, what would it take for you to become engaged?

Sometimes, you learn the most about yourself when you least expect to. I used these questions with a colleague. She started to write her answers to these questions and realized she was looking for the "same old job." She didn't want the same old job. She wanted a new and different job. That was why she wasn't engaged with her job search. She was now ready to answer the third question.

Now it's time to answer, "What would you like to have happen?" This might prompt you to answer for yourself, "What does success look like for me?"

Maybe you need to Define Your Purpose, p. 64.

3.8 Use Five Whys

If you think you have another reason for many open ToDos, try a root cause analysis tool called the "Five Whys." You ask the question Why at least four times—preferably five—to understand the root cause of the problem. Here's how one colleague diagnosed his problem:

"Why did you have so many tasks in your "In Progress" column?" (First why)

"Because I procrastinated on doing them."

"Why did you procrastinate on doing them?" (Second why)

"Because I was afraid of doing them."

"Why were you afraid of doing them?" (Third why. There was a long pause here.)

"Because I don't want to discover that there are no jobs for me."

"Why don't you want to discover there are no jobs in your field?" (Fourth why)

"Because then I will have to do something else, I guess."

"Why will you have to do something else? (Fifth why)

"Because I have to provide for my family or die trying!"

When you find yourself in this place, it's because you are imagining the Worst Thing That Could Happen, p. 131. You need to do risk management.

Make no mistake about it. Our jobs, type of employment, and our self-esteem are tied together in a Gordian knot. Your approach to your job search can reflect your self-esteem. If you erect barriers, you will get in your own way. So, see if you are a barrier-erector. Too much work in progress during a given week can be a barrier to your progress.

You might be worried. What is the first step you can take to make forward progress? Is it asking for an informational interview? Is it connecting with someone on LinkedIn?

The "Five Whys" help you see where you are stuck. Now, you can help yourself get unstuck. Find three small ToDos. Make sure they are small. Put them on your "Ready To Do" column.

For the next week, commit to doing them. What is the worst thing that can happen? You're already managing your project so you have small deliverables, looking at your progress, and problem-solving along the way. I have suggestions for you, if you are in Special Circumstances, p. 159. You have many ways to manage risk.

Do you feel as if you have Impostor Syndrome, that you cannot repeat your past successes? See Managing Impostor Syndrome, p. 123.

Do you have rules about jobs? I have suggestions for you, too. See Perfection Rules Trap Us Every Time, p. 121.

Are you fresh out of ideas? Use the Rule of Three for Generating More Ideas, p. 139.

Consider drawing a mindmap of your week, which is the topic of the next section.

Your job is to maintain your self-esteem and congruence, while managing your job search project. It's a tough job. I'm with you.

3.9 Draw a MindMap of Your Week

A mindmap is a visual outline of information. Because it's a visual thinking tool, it has the possibility of providing you with different information than the other reflection tools.

In a mind map, you start with a central idea, your job hunt. You draw branches off that central idea, capturing the important ideas that occurred during the week.

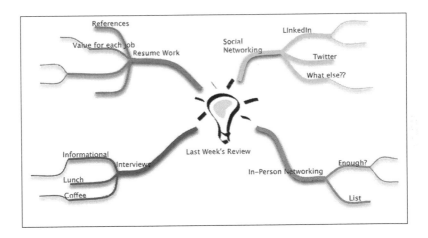

Think of this mind map as a prototype for you to consider, not copy. You can find free software online at MindMeister[1], MindMup[2], or FreeMind[3]. I drew this mindmap with Omnigraffle[4]. And, paper and pen work too.

---

[1]http://www,mindmeister.com

[2]http://www.mindmup.com

[3]http://freemind.sourceforge.net

[4]http://www.omnigraffle.com

With a mind map, you might decide to ask other people for feedback about your map. You might even decide to build on the map week after week, to have a more holistic view of your job search.

Create another view of your search, using a different modality.

3.10 Now Do This

1. How much did you accomplish this week? Can you do more? Should you do less? Are you comfortable with the amount of work you're doing?

2. Can you reflect alone or do you need someone to reflect with you? Many of us need help reflecting. When I started my consulting business, I asked my husband and close colleagues for regular help reflecting. You might consider asking for help, too.

3. Which of the reflection approaches help you most? Do you know why?

CHAPTER 4

Iterate and Organize

You want to use what you've learned to iterate on *everything*, to maintain a sustainable pace and to apply the principles of flow to your work.

You understand the basics now: plan just a little, enough for a week. Visualize and track your work. Reflect on your work and use your reflection to plan for the next week. You can use this for the big tasks of your job search:

- Network, network, network. Can you use LinkedIn, Twitter, maybe even FaceBook, Google+, whatever the next social medium is, for your job search? Your job search is not just about *what* you know. Your job search is about who you know and how people will find you.
- Create, update, and tweak your résumé. Think about where to place your résumé so internal recruiters, hiring managers, and external recruiters can find you.
- Apply for jobs.
- Ask for recommendations and references. If you have solid experience working with people, offer recommendations and references, too.
- Interview feedback. You can ask for feedback about your interview style, especially if you've built rapport with a hiring manager.

If you have a big task, you can timebox it. Maybe you want to set a one-hour timebox for investigating a company or a job fair.

When You Do Something Good Enough for Now, p. 140, you have an opportunity to do something else, and continue to make progress. When you don't have too much work in progress or too many big chunks of work, this will enable you to accomplish more. When you combine these two approaches, you have a powerful approach for a complex project, such as finding a new job.

I have some tips for your résumé in Write Your Résumé, p. 67. And, when it comes to tweaking your résumé, I recommend Andy Lester's book, *Land the Tech Job You Love* (LES09). He covers that topic in much better detail than I can here.

The networking chapter, Network, Network, Network, p. 101 provides many tips about networking. In addition, the chapter Use Social Media to Network, p. 113 discusses the basics of LinkedIn and Twitter for networking.

You'll want to iterate on both your résumé and your networking as you search for your next job.

4.1 Plan Your Next One-Week Timebox

You reviewed your previous week's work and noticed two critical pieces of data: how much work in progress you had (your WIP); and how many ToDos you completed. You can plan the next week based on those two pieces of data. Don't assume you can do more than you did last week—that way lies disaster. Why? Because you are going to set your expectations too high.

Assume you can do what you did last week *if*, and only *if*, you were happy with the quality of your work. If you think you rushed through too many ToDos just to finish them, you have some choices:

- You can choose to finish fewer tasks.
- You can break down your ToDos into more tasks that are smaller.
- You can attach criteria to your tasks so you know when you are really done.

- You might need to use "The Pen" more often than for just callbacks.
- Use "The Pen" for the interdependent work, too.

If you got through everything last week, and had time left over, terrific! That's a good reason to plan to do more for this coming week.

As you did for the first week, write your stickies, keeping them small enough to complete in a couple of hours or less; and make them as independent as possible. Did work arise during the week? That's fine. As work arises, make a sticky so you can track it and its progress. Make sure you maintain a handle on your WIP.

Review your Parking Lot. Do you want to move any of the stickies you had on your Parking Lot to your "Ready To Do" list for ranking? If so, do that now. See what you can accomplish this week. Do not attempt to plan more than you can do in a week.

Keep doing this: planning, executing the small ToDos, watching your WIP so you don't have too much in progress at any one time. That will prevent you from being overwhelmed by the enormity of your job search.

And, every so often, celebrate your successes. You've earned them.

4.2 Organize Your Email, Electronic Folders, and Physical Folders

One of the challenges in a job search is that you have tons of email, many versions or iterations of your résumé, and many potential employers. You need to organize all of these electronic documents so you know where everything is. You might not discover your "perfect" organization your first week.

Do not worry. You can also iterate on your organization.

 There is no perfect organization. You only need a *good-enough* organization so you don't lose anything. Do not make yourself berserk organizing. Do not spend time organizing when you can spend time finding a job.

These are my suggestions for organizing so you can be successful in your job search. You don't have to do this. I offer this to you only as a starting point, so you can iterate and make whatever you do work for you.

4.2.1 *Organize Your Email*

First, organize your email. You will need to know what you *sent* to people.

I keep all my sent email in my "sent" folder each month. At the end of the month, I copy it into a folder that corresponds to a specific year and month. For every year, I have twelve folders: Jan, Feb, Mar, Apr, May, etc. Each of those months has the corresponding "sent" email in it. I can always search the sent email by date sent. Am I a little crazy? Maybe. However, I like to know when I have sent which email to whom. My attachments are in my email, so I can see them.

Now, you still have to manage your inbox. Although I aspire to Inbox Zero[1], I have yet to achieve it.

What I do is process every email I can, when I can. The big things, the ones I can't process and delete, go on my ToDo list. I recommend you do something similar.

I have a LinkedIn folder and filters in my email so I can process LinkedIn email separately from my Inbox. That might work for you, too.

You will be spending much of your time in email, so use filters and rules to categorize and filter your email.

You might want a specific job-hunting email address, especially if your personal email is "lovestoski@gmail.com." Hiring managers might think you'd rather ski than work. And, you do want to place your best professional foot forward. Consider using a more professional email name when you look for a job.

4.2.2 *Organize Your Résumé Folders*

Next, organize your résumé folder or folders. Do you have several versions of your résumé out for review? Do you have one slanted for

---

[1]http://www.inboxzero.com

a technical leadership role and one as a business analyst or one as a technical writer and one as a developer? If you are flexible about the position you seek, you might have several different résumés. Maintain different folders, so you know where your *current* up-to-date résumé is.

Make sure you have a résumé in doc, text, and pdf formats. Yes, companies might ask for all of these formats. Give them what they ask for. It doesn't matter if you don't like it. You are the candidate. You give them what they want.

4.2.3 *Organize Your Tracking Information*

Last, you want to organize how you will track the companies and recruiters to whom you submit résumés. You might maintain a spreadsheet. If you prefer, you might keep a database. You need to track the company name, the date you submitted the information, the job number, and any other relevant information, such as whether it was an employee referral. If it was an employee referral, track who the employee was. You need this information if you want to follow up. Or—if the company calls you back after six months. It happens.

4.2.4 *Organize Your Contact Information*

You are meeting, or are planning to meet, all these nice people as you network. You'll be meeting some of them online, some in person. You'll want to track when and how you met them.

I track people in my Contacts application on my Mac. I add two fields: When I met the person, and Where I met the person. That application already has company name and phone number as part of the application.

How will you remember to call people? If you need a reminder *this* week, it goes into your ToDos or The Pen. Otherwise, I make a reminder or an appointment in my Calendar application to remind me to do something on a particular day. You could also make a sticky and add it to your Parking Lot for a specific day.

Whatever you do, write it down somewhere so you don't have to remember it.

4.3 Iterate on Your Organization

Don't spend any more time on organization than the bare-bones I've suggested. You want to see what works and what doesn't work for *you.* Maybe you need more information in your tracking information than I've suggested. Maybe you process email differently.

What works for me might not work for you. You need to discover what works for you.

4.4 Now Do This

1. Do you know where you need to iterate?
2. Are your tasks independent or interdependent? If you have many interdependent tasks, see if you can break them apart. It's worth your time to spend a little more time planning one day so you spend the rest of your week breezing through the work.
3. Do you have interim milestones where you can celebrate?

It's time to start thinking about how you will iterate and where. Are you happy with your networking? With your feedback? With your interviewing? Use your reflection to decide on your experiments for the upcoming week.

PART II

Choosing a Career, Interviewing, and Deciding on an Offer

Sometimes, I meet people, and they say, "JR, I just don't know what to do. I have a BA in Philosophy. I could do anything. I'm a critical thinker!" Or, "I have 20 years of development experience. I could do just about any job in development. But, I have no idea what to do." Or, "I've been out of the job market for ten years, but I am so organized, I could do anything. How do I get a potential employer to give me a chance?"

What makes you want to go to work in the morning? What does a great job look like for you? How will you know you've found it?

CHAPTER 5
Know Your Previous Job Patterns

If you are looking for a job, it's important that you know what your previous patterns are, so that you can make a choice: Do I repeat my previous patterns this time? Without knowing what our patterns are, we tend to repeat them. Once we know, we have choices.

One of the best ways I know how to do this is with a career timeline.

Take a piece of paper that is sufficiently large for your career. When I run workshops I ask people to take a piece of flipchart paper and turn it landscape. A regular piece of paper or two pieces taped together might work if you've been in the workplace for a while. Make sure the paper is in landscape mode, not portrait.

Now, the X axis is time, and the Y axis is satisfaction and/or happiness. The middle of the paper is the neutral line, the top of the paper is the most satisfied you can ever imagine being and the bottom is the least satisfied you can ever imagine being. You are going to make a career timeline of your career, including the plotting of your major career and/or personal lifetime achievements on the X axis. You have at least two ways to do this:

1. You can plot the major events first, and then draw how you felt: the ups and downs before and after the events up until the present day.
2. You can make a continuous line, noting the major events.
3. There is probably a third way I haven't considered. Be my guest and let me know what you did, so I can include it as an option!

The idea is that we have patterns of behavior that we repeat. My patterns are not your patterns. Your colleagues' patterns are not your patterns. No one has patterns that are just like yours.

Nobody's career is linear. I don't know a single person who planned a career and then had their career move linearly upwards. Most people have careers that move up, down, sideways, up, sideways, down, up, and other variations. If you thought your career should always be moving up, up, up, think again. It's fine to take a step sideways or down. I have. Most people do. The ones who say they haven't are either confused, mistaken, or—possibly lying.

This should take you a while. The first time I drew my career timeline, it took me about an hour. I missed a few things. You don't want to miss anything. If you think it's too much for one sitting, start now, and iterate. That way you can make progress on other pieces of your job search.

5.1 Start with Your First Job

Where do you start? With your first job. When was your first job? When *you* chose your first job. Why am I being vague? Because I don't know if you considered babysitting or mowing lawns your first job. Do you? Then include it.

I considered my first job the one when I graduated from college, not the factory jobs in high school or the programming job or the operator job in college. Why? Because those jobs were not full time and did not showcase my, ahem, sterling qualities. If your teenage jobs *did* showcase your sterling qualities, then, please, do include them. Some of us, like me, took a little longer to season. If in doubt, start with your first *full-time* job.

If you are a recent grad, start with your very *first* job. Yes, your very first job, whether that was an unpaid babysitting job for your parents when you were 12, or that unpaid internship last year.

So, are you with me now? You have taken the time to chart your career. You have noted the major events and drawn how you *felt* about those events. Now is the time to mine your career line for its goodies.

5.2 Mine Your Career Line

Step back and look at your career line. Look for patterns. What do you see? Do you see some common ups and downs?

Talk with yourself, pair with someone, or use a trusted advisor. When I look at my career line, I noticed some common patterns. For example, when I get bored or have no work, I get unhappy and look for a job. When the work is not in my control, I get unhappy and look for a job. My values are learning, challenge, and control over my job.

Consider these questions:

- How did you discover this job? Did you network to find your job? How deeply?
- What did you like about the job before you started? What were your expectations? How closely did your expectations match reality?
- Why did you leave? Was it a culture fit? Was it something different?

You have some other questions to ponder:

- What circumstances provided you the most satisfaction in this job?
- What patterns do you tend to create for yourself?
- How did you feel while doing your career line?
- How do you react to positive events? To negative ones?

Your career timeline will look something like this:

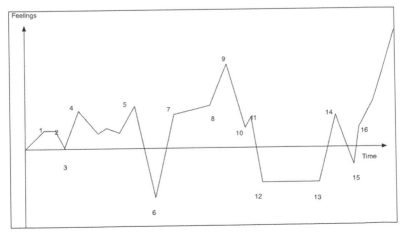

I have my career timeline annotated with numbers. When I lead workshops, I discuss what those numbers mean. For example, #3 is when I had nothing to do. I was down because I was bored, but not seriously down.

The time between 12 and 13, I was at a job that was wrong for me and I knew it. That was a *long* time to be at a job that was wrong.

Because by nature I'm a positive person, I don't spend lots of time below the neutral line, so I would have to explain the line to you. I made this line back in 2006, so it doesn't have the most recent years on it.

The key is that you look for what causes the ups and downs. You look for your patterns. Not every up or down is a job change. It's an up or a down. You want to know what causes the ups and downs, and then what prompts you to change jobs.

I once saw a career line that looked like this:

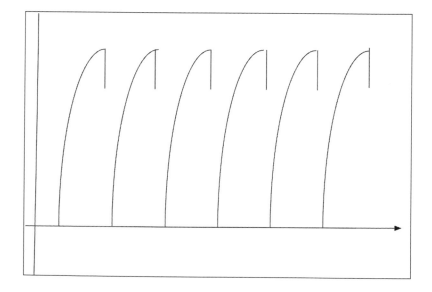

This is a person who repeats one particular pattern, again and again. It is useful to know this pattern. You can always make a choice to continue this pattern. You might make a choice to break this pattern.

This person preemptively left before anything really bad could happen. His expectations were so high that anything could look bad. We discussed this and he had some ideas about moderating his expectations and not leaving companies right away.

I learned about this technique in Gerald Weinberg's *Becoming a Technical Leader* (WEI86).

5.3 What Did You Learn From Your Career Line?

What did you learn from your career timeline? What patterns do you repeat? What words do you use over and over again to describe your reactions to your career and to your life?

There are some patterns in my life. I need to have fun in a job, keep learning, and to have control over my work. You'll notice there is nothing about safety or risk in my description of what's important to me. No wonder I became a consultant! This is why everyone's patterns are different and why I can't tell you what's important to you. But I bet your career timeline will tell you what is important to you.

When you describe the ups and downs in your career, you articulate the cultural values that are important to you, or the cultural environment that you cannot work in. The ups are the values that are important. The downs are indicative of the values that do not resonate with you.

Make sure you spend enough time discussing this. Do not shortchange this. If you find this uncomfortable, try several small timeboxes of 20 minutes, spread over several days. You don't have to analyze it all at once.

This might be important enough to you to ask for feedback from a trusted colleague, mentor, friend, or spouse. Maybe, even all of the above. If you are working with a career coach, ask that person, too. If you use your career timeline to change how you look for a job, you will want feedback on your changes.

5.4 What Culture Do You Want in a New Job?

Believe it or not, that knowledge is in your career timeline. Now it's time to think about the culture you want in a job.

5.4.1 *Set Boundaries About Discussions*

Start with your most recent job. Think back to some conversations you had that made you happy with your boss and with your colleagues that were about work. What did those conversations have in common? List three things. Those are three things that were great. You want to keep them in mind. Those are things you want to be able to talk about at work. For example, I want to be able to talk about how a company makes—or is in danger of *not* making money. I want those conversations to be open and above-board.

Think back to some conversations that made you uncomfortable or made you say, "Huh?" or "What is going on here?" List three things either in the content of the conversation or about the conversation. I personally don't want to be subject to "jokes" about different ethnicities, or kinds of people, or women. To me, those are not jokes, they are prejudices and put-downs. They're not funny. They are beyond my boundary of what's okay to talk about.

Now you have three things that are okay to talk about and three things that are not okay to talk about. Those things you weren't comfortable talking about? They could be clues about how people are treated at work, too.

5.4.2 *Set Boundaries About How the Organization Treats You*

Now, how have you been treated at your past job? Did you have one-on-ones with your manager? Did you receive feedback and career guidance every week? Did you have collegial relationships with people you worked closely with? Are those things important to you? What else might be important to you? Take your time and list at least three other things that are important to you. Take your time. I know I said that. This is an important step. You don't have to rush.

Now, list three things that are anti-patterns for you, things that will drive you away from a culture. I don't mean the paint on the walls, I mean things that will drive you away from an organization. Is it a manager canceling a one-on-one? Is it someone who doesn't understand continuous integration and won't learn? (Gee, guess what's important to me?)

5.4.3 *Set Boundaries About Rewards*

The reward step is next. Once we are paid enough to get money off the negotiating table, we don't work for money. (See Daniel Pink's *Drive: The Surprising Truth About What Motivates Us* (PIN09).) Many of us in software work for recognition by our peers, but not all of us. Some of us work for a promotion. Some work to accumulate people "under" us. If you want a paternal organization, you want to find a company like that. Me, I ran away from companies like that. What do you work for? Again, take your time and list three things that are important to you.

Now, list three things that the company might have done to reward people that just made you nuts. One of my companies a long time ago had an Engineer-of-the-Year award. They only gave it to developers. I was a tester. They only gave it to men. I was (and still am) a woman. They only gave it to single men. I was (and still am) married. Did they think I wouldn't notice? They gave it at the company Christmas party. It was so noticeably one-sided that I wasn't the only one who noticed. Several people thought I was going to be rewarded because of my efforts on a particular release. It looked like I had been snubbed.

Here I am, almost 30 years later, and I still feel the anger. Wow. That's a lot of emotion about a job long gone. That company didn't recognize me for my efforts. And, I liked working there!

So, list the kind of recognition/reward efforts the company has made that doesn't fit your style. I'm not saying you will find the perfect company. I am saying that with your lists you can find something that fits you more, rather than less.

5.4.4 *Gather Your Lists*

You now have six lists:

- Three things you enjoyed talking about at work
- Three things you shook your head about, or made you say, "Huh, what is going on here?"
- Three things that you enjoyed about how the organization/managers treated you
- Three things about the organization that made you crazy, that drove you away from the organization
- Three things about rewards or recognition that attracted you to the organization
- Three things about rewards or recognition that turned you off

These are the things that reflect the culture of the organization. It's time for you to create questions you can ask before or during the interview, so you know the job is right for you.

5.5 Create Questions You Can Ask About Cultural Fit in the Interview

Decide which questions are most important. For example, I hate mandatory fun, such as holiday parties. Just hate them. You, on the other hand, might adore them. Aren't you glad we are different people?

Even though I dislike them, it's not a make-or-break thing for the company. It is part of the overall picture.

Here's how I'll craft the question. First, I'll use a closed question to see what the organization does, and if the answer is yes, ask for more data:

Do you have company parties for holidays? . . . Under what circumstances?

Are people required or encouraged to dress in costume for parties like Halloween?

Notice that I leave my emotional reaction out of it. I am asking for data. Just ask for data. No leading questions. If the answer is yes, I'll let the interviewer lead, and go where the interview takes me.

Now, I feel very strongly about not collecting for charity or pushing political organizations at work. I'll ask the same kind of questions:

Do you have a United Way or other charitable campaign here?

We had a really active political season in 2011. Do you have a policy on politics at the office?

I was consulting to a bank in one of the election years when Bush-the-younger was running. A very senior manager was wearing a Bankers-for-Bush button, and Bush paraphernalia was all over his office. He asked me point-blank if I was voting for Bush. I told him it was none of his business. He told me Bush was good for banks. I told him I was voting for the good of the country. I asked him if he was using his position to tell his people how to vote. He said, "Heck, yes!" I explained that was not a good use of his managerial power and might be illegal.

Your questions might be about meetings (how many) or continuous integration (how do you do it here) or testing (tell me how you do testing here).

When you ask questions about the things that make you crazy, you want to ask for data first. When you ask questions such as "Tell me how you do continuous integration here," you are making an assumption that people know what CI is. This gives them the benefit of the doubt, which is a *nice* thing to do. You have also turned this into a behavior-description question. You can then ask, "How did CI work on your most recent project?" Same thing with testing, or any other practice that you've noticed made you crazy at a previous job.

Do you see how asking for data, these closed questions, start a conversation? They often get you just enough information. Especially if you have your list of questions.

5.6 **When Do You Ask About Culture?**

You have opportunities to ask questions about culture in the phone screen and in the in-person interview. You can try to learn about the culture from the ad, but that's a little more difficult. There is no guarantee that the hiring manager or team wrote the ad, or that the ad represents the culture.

During the interview, you have the opportunity to learn about the culture in these ways:

- When you meet the receptionist, or whether there is a receptionist
- When you meet each interviewer, and definitely at the end of the interview with each person. See Ask Questions of the Hiring Manager, p. 84 and the Interview Team.
- If you have a meal with anyone, during the meal
- When you meet the HR person
- After the interview, you have more opportunities:
- When they call to set up another interview
- When someone calls to check references

Let's look at each of these.

5.6.1 *Ask Questions Before the Interview*

During the phone screen, if you have great rapport with the interviewer, consider asking one or two questions. I would not ask more than one or two questions. And, only about something that has burned you more than once. If you thought you were working for an agile organization, and the last two were not agile, you might ask, "Do you do standups every day? Maybe we can schedule my interview so I can see your standup."

Notice how I framed that question. If the interviewer notices that you are not taking anything for granted, you can explain that you have noticed that some so-called agile organizations don't have standups every day, and you want to make sure they do.

Whatever you do, do not pass judgment before you get in the door. You have no idea where these folks started and what they managed to accomplish. You can choose to take the interview or not. And, you always have another decision point after the first interview.

5.6.2 *Ask Questions During the Interview*

Now you have many more options. You can ask the receptionist questions. Maybe you noticed there are assigned parking spaces for "employee of the month." Ask how those are assigned. I bet the receptionist will tell you. This is how people are rewarded, a big part of culture.

When you meet with people, have your questions ready. If you must, have them on a piece of paper, that you can pull out of your pocket. When you meet with different people, ask each one a different question, at the end of your allotted time. Again, make this a judgment-free zone. You are asking out of curiosity, not putting people on the spot. You want to know why they like working here.

If you have a chance to eat a meal with people, this is great. I like to ask this question, "What is great about working here?" a meta-question. People fall over themselves, answering this question. You will hear all kinds of things. And, you get to eat your meal, which is great.

If you meet with the HR person, you can ask other questions. It really depends on how savvy the HR person is. Some HR people don't know much about the group you will be working with. They know about the corporation. So, they can't tell you much about the group's culture, which is what you really want to know. Remember, every team and every manager puts its stamp on the corporate culture. Ask questions. And, use your judgment about which questions to ask.

5.6.3 *Ask Questions After the First Interview*

If you didn't take advantage of asking too many questions at the first interview, you should at any second-round or other interview.

Remember, the interview is for both the hiring manager/team and you. Don't interrogate people. Do take advantage of your greater rapport with the hiring manager to ask questions.

5.6.4 *Ask Questions After all the Interviews*

When the hiring manager calls for your references, provide the references. This is late to be asking questions. You should not have any doubts left. And, if you do, ask your questions. Taking a new job is a big commitment. If you have questions, ask.

Make sure to ask your questions from a sense of curiosity. Don't judge your potential hiring manager and team. Not without obtaining the facts. Use follow-up questions to learn the facts.

Start with closed questions to learn about data. Use behavior-description questions to learn about recent projects. Try meta-questions to learn about the question, about the organization.

5.7 Define Your Purpose

Do you know what you want to do? If you don't know what you want to do, first, define your purpose.

When you define your purpose, some people think, "I must be the next great 'insert some famous person's name here.'" Maybe. I have found it more useful to be the best *me* that I can be.

Especially if you're in transition, ask yourself these questions:

1. What do you do? What do you love to do? What is the one thing you feel supremely qualified to teach other people?
2. Who do you do it for?
3. What do those people want or need?
4. How do they change or transform as a result of what you give them?

Notice that these are outward facing questions. They help you articulate your value to other people, especially hiring managers.

These questions are from Adam Leipzig's TED Talk, How to Know Your Life Purpose in 5 Minutes (LEI13). These questions work if you have been working for a while. They might not work if you are a recent grad, or if you are in transition.

If you are unseasoned in a career, maybe you don't have a purpose yet. Choose something. Here are some resources that might help you select a path.

- Tom Rath has written a book called *Strengths Finder 2.0* (RAT07), where you take an online assessment. You read the book to examine your strengths, and then decide if you are working to your strengths, or would be better off in a different role.
- If you're not already technical, consider going to code.org[1] and see if you like programming. (Yes, I am a one-woman band for helping people move into technical fields, such as software. I realize software is not for everyone.)
- Consider working with a career coach to help you understand what your purpose is, for now.

Your job, when you are unseasoned, is to gain great experience, so you can decide what your purpose is.

5.8 Define What Success Looks Like For You

Many people talk about finding their passion. That's great, if you know what your passion is. If you were very lucky, you discovered your passion early. If you are like the rest of us, yes, me included, you did not.

If you generated your career timeline, you saw that your career is not linear. No one's is.

But, you can know what success looks like for you in a job. Success is something that fits your cultural needs, that provides you with enough money to live on, and fulfills your purpose in life—for

---

[1]http://www.code.org

now. Your definition of success may very well change as you change throughout your life. That's great.

Here are some questions for you to consider:

- What would a day in a great job look like?
- What is this worth to me?
- What would make me say yes to an offer?
- What would make me say no to an offer?

Imagine what a day in a great job would be like for you. Is it going to an office? Working on the road? With a team? Alone? Some combination of the above?

How about what it's worth to you? Do you have a family whose needs you must consider when you take a new job? Does that mean that a relocation is possible or not? How about if you have to travel? Or, if the job is just outside your comfort zone for a commute? Could they pay you enough to move? Or commute? Or travel?

If you think about what success looks like now, at the beginning of your job search, you will be self-assured, relaxed, and willing to negotiate. You will know what you want. Now you are ready to write your résumé.

5.9 **Now Do This**

1. Make your own timeline, first draft. Give yourself plenty of time to do this. I allocate 45 minutes to two hours. Annotate it, so you know what job is where, and what other events in your life occurred that might have affected your timeline.
2. If you can, find someone else to discuss your timeline with. When you discuss it, what do you notice you *say*, about your timeline? What are the words that you use to discuss your career?
3. Those words are the cultural-fit words for a potential employer. How will you use those words to look for a job in the future?

CHAPTER 6

Write Your Résumé

You need a résumé that represents you for every job you apply for.

6.1 Do I Need an Objective on My Résumé?

Do you need an objective? No, unless it's going to say something other than "Desire a challenging position." Everyone desires a challenging position. Don't bother with that.

But if you are changing positions, and you want to highlight that change, yes, say something about that. If you've been a technical lead and you want to be a manager, say that. If you've been a manager and you want to be a technical lead, say that. If you've been in high tech and you want to be a teacher, say that. That's what an objective is good for—when you want a change and you need to highlight the change.

6.2 Specify the Dates of Each Position in Reverse Chronological Order

Start with your most recent position first. I like to read résumés where the left column is the month/year to month/year of the job, and the next column tells me the position and what you did. I find those résumés easy to read.

If you have a different style of résumé, make sure you have a darn good reason. If you took time off for some reason and you want to highlight some previous experience, that *might* be a good reason. But, I can add. I can see when you have and have not worked. Address your experience or lack thereof in a cover letter. Don't write a strange résumé that makes me hunt for your information.

6.3 Insert Technical Skills and Education Last

If you are looking for a knowledge work position, make sure you highlight your experience with your value. See Explain the Value of Every Item on Your Résumé, p. 69. This will take time, so make sure you provide enough time to think through the value of each position.

For your first draft résumé, insert your skills last on your résumé, and go back to your value. Keep refining the value. It will be easier to add all your applications and technical skills than it will be to add your value. It's fine to add your technical skills and education while you think about them, but make them last.

6.4 Keep Your Résumé to Two Pages

Here's a guideline: your résumé should be no longer than two pages, three at the outside. Why? So a hiring manager can read it quickly. You don't have much time to impress a hiring manager. Make the most of it.

You can't make your résumé and cover letter say everything about you. You still need something to discuss at the interview.

Say you've been working for more than 20 years. How do you do this? Well, only the most recent 10 years is important. The rest can be grouped together. Remember, you can refer people to your LinkedIn page for more detail. Or, if you have an online résumé page, you can refer people to that.

Do you know about about.me?[1] For now, at least, it's a free service that allows you to create personalized web pages. You can add your personal page at about.me, insert a link on your résumé, and point your readers to that page if you need to create more pages and you don't have a website.

---

[1]https://about.me/

If you have significant accomplishments, you want to keep them on your résumé. There are some items you do not want to leave off your paper résumé:

- Patents
- Books
- Honors
- Awards
- Publications

If you have many of any of the above, you can refer people to a page on your website, or to your LinkedIn profile. If I say "author of several books, 2 more upcoming, see this URL for more information," that's enough.

The most important things about you are how you work at work, how you take responsibility, how you take initiative, how you work with your colleagues, *not* what you wrote. How do you learn and how quickly do you learn? How do you work with people? How do you deliver?

6.4.1 *Explain the Value of Every Item on Your Résumé*

Your technical skills are important. But what's *most* important about you are your talents: your qualities, preferences, non-technical skills. The way you talk about it is to discuss it in terms of the value you bring to your employer. I like the way Rich Stone wrote it down in Value Action Method: Explain the Value[2].

For every line on your résumé, explain the value. If your build system automation work on a project saved three-person weeks every quarter, you would say something like this:

Saved three person-weeks every quarter via automation by delivering scripts for the build system

---

[2]http://insearchof.regenerateweb.net/resume-and-interview-preparation-tips/

That's still a little wimpy. As a first draft, that might be good enough. If this is your first week, maybe you stop there. However, if you are refining your résumé, or you haven't worked for too long, you want to craft each line on your résumé. How can you clarify this line to specify your value?

Saved three person-weeks every quarter by automating scripts for our git-based build system. We transitioned from SVN to git and I automated the scripts.

Anyone who knows anything about version control will now understand what you did and will be able to ask you questions. You've written this in English—well, abbreviated English, and you have something to discuss in the interview.

Let's try another example which is a little less technical. Maybe you're a project manager. Project managers tend to facilitate and coordinate. Sometimes, it's difficult to articulate a project manager's value, especially if you're not a command-and-control project manager.

Led a program to integrate all the platforms into one suite of software. I coordinated 10 distributed technical teams in three time zones over 14 months. We released internally to verify our deliverables with our sponsors as a risk management effort four times (not agile, but not waterfall). We released to high customer acclaim and notable press and media coverage. Our support costs decreased 80%. Revenue increased 50% in the first quarter.

With such great success, you will have to explain why you are looking for a new job.

This is difficult. You want to use numbers as much as possible. Use sentences. Read them out loud and see if they make sense.

If it's hard for you to write down, chances are good that you are articulating your value. See Andy Lester's *Land the Tech Job You Love* for more helpful tips about your résumé (LES09).

6.5 Never Lie on a Résumé

Never lie on your résumé. Never expand the truth a little bit. Never fake it. It's too easy for other people to check on your résumé's facts. If you went to Harvard and didn't graduate, say "attended Harvard." That's it. Never lie.

I attended MIT as a special student for three classes. I don't even put that on my résumé. It would raise more questions than it would settle. Sure, MIT is a prestigious institution, but I never got a degree, I just studied there for three classes. It's not worth the aggravation of trying to explain what I did. It doesn't go on my résumé.

Never lie or even stretch the truth. When it matters professionally, someone will discover it and you will be in trouble. Don't do it.

6.6 Don't List Reference Names on Your Résumé

You might want different references for different positions. And, you want to provide your references with advance warning that someone will be calling when you have a hot job, one that is close to an offer.

You do want to say "References on request," somewhere on the résumé or in the cover letter.

6.7 Ask People to be References

When you ask people to be your references, make sure you ask for their work phone number, home phone number, and as many email addresses as they are able to provide. Some reference checkers prefer email-only checks. Some reference checkers prefer phone only. Ask your reference what *their* preference is, and explain that to the reference checker.

You should have at least three references. Select at least two managers and one peer. If you have three managers, that's better. Of course, it also depends on how long ago those references worked with you. If those references are very old, what they have to say may not seem relevant to your current potential hiring managers. Look for people who will be relevant.

Ask the reference what they would say about working with you again. If they would *not* work with you again, don't use that person as a reference. Find someone else. Or, understand the circumstances, so you can prepare the reference checker.

Here's an email that one of my readers sent to one of his references:

Joe,

As you know I'm currently looking for a full-time job and going on interviews. You may have received a reference-check call or email inquiring about me in the past few months from other recruiters. I would like to formalize my references list and I hope I can count on your support moving forward.

I found a couple local jobs that look very promising and am in the process of interviewing for them. In the interview process, I'm going to be asked for references. I have thought about the people I've worked with over the past few years and you are one of the 3 people for whom I have the highest regard in my professional life. I know that you are very busy. I would like to give the recruiters your email address and ask that they first contact you via email and, if they need to speak to you (which they probably will) that they provide their own phone number and ask you to call them back at your convenience.

One concern I have is that we're in a challenging "buyer's" market. I usually don't have a 100% match for all the posted requirements so you may be asked about a skill that I don't yet have or you're not aware of. That's OK. Just let them know that I've demonstrated that I pick up new frameworks and technologies quickly. Hopefully they'll find value in that response.

I will be happy to return the favor if you are looking for either a job or a business reference for a contract in the future. Thank you for being there for me and I still hope we can work together again in a future venture. Let me know if you have any concerns.

Thanks, Happy Holidays, and best of luck for a prosperous new year!

I het you noticed a few things in this email. My reader is preparing the reference to be asked, and how he will be asked. The "first contact via email" is a request. It might not survive, but my reader is letting his reference know he has made the request.

He's also addressing the reality that he might not have a "100% match" for all the requirements. But he does remind the reference that he learns quickly. That's a nice touch.

Also, notice how he offers to pay the request forward, by helping Joe find a job, be a reference, or working together in the future.

Consider using this kind of an email or note for your references. You won't use the same language. You'll want to emphasize something different. Maybe you want to emphasize your ability to coordinate across the organization, or your design skills, or your language skills, or something entirely different. But this is how you ask people to be your reference.

Who would say no? Only someone you don't want.

6.8 Iterate on Your Résumé Several Times

Your résumé is the same as any other piece of writing. You should expect to draft it and send it out for review several times.

If you are thinking of applying for different types of jobs, you might even want different kinds of résumés. Each of those résumés will need drafts and review.

Take your time. Look for inconsistencies and typos. Some hiring managers toss résumés when they see a typo.

- Are you capitalizing properly? This includes computer languages and tools. If you're not sure, look it up. Fortran is now spelled with just one capital letter. It used to be spelled FORTRAN. MATLAB is all caps. Know how to spell your tools, regardless of your industry.
- Is your title spelled the way your company spells it? Yes, some of you are called "principle" engineers. You and I both know

you should be called "principal" engineers. I give up. Just spell it the way your company spells it.

- Use a spell-checker. Use a grammar-checker on your sentences. You don't have to use buzzword bingo on your résumé.

Remember that you want to make your résumé easy to read. A hiring manager may or may not see your cover letter. The manager will see your résumé. You have up to 30 seconds to make a good impression.

6.9 Create Several Versions of Your Résumé

You will need several versions of your résumé: at least in doc format and in pdf. You may need other formats, such as plain text, so be ready.

I don't care if you don't like doc format. If that's what the HR or hiring manager wants, that's what you provide.

You want to provide pdf, because no one has to see whether you used styles correctly or not. When you pdf a document, all they can see is the final output.

6.10 Now Do This

1. Review your résumé from the big-picture standpoint. How long is it? Can a hiring manager read it in a couple of minutes?
2. For every line on your résumé, have you articulated your value on your résumé with numbers or some other detail?
3. Did you write the most important information on the front? Did you save the (long) list of obligatory technical skills for the back?

CHAPTER 7

Prepare for the Interview

You've landed an interview. You have a customized cover letter with your résumé. On your résumé, you've summarized your experience in reverse chronological order, maybe including an objective. On your résumé, you've:

1. Highlighted any real-world work experience
2. Showed how you applied your learned skills to the real world
3. Included your tools experience last

In the interview, your job is to answer questions well, ask good questions, and choose references that will help you close the job. What else do you need to do?

7.1 Know How Much Time You Need for the Interview

When the hiring manager or HR rep asks you to come in for an interview, ask how much time you should expect to spend in the interview. Now, add more time.

You want to be ready for commuting time, and for additional time if the interview is proceeding well. You want flexibility if they love you and you want to talk to more people. And, since you don't normally commute to that location, you want to allow plenty of time to arrive at that location.

7.2 **Know Where You're Going**

I bet most of you rely on your GPS for driving directions. Well, don't only rely on your GPS. Make sure you have a paper map backup of your directions. That way, if your GPS is wrong—wow, that's never happened, has it?—you can look at a map and know where to go. If you're really risk averse, do a drive-by or a commute-by the day before.

Does this seem like overkill to you? It depends on whether you really want the job or not, doesn't it?

Allow plenty of time to arrive at the interview. You can always sit in the lobby. But, if you arrive late, you'll feel rushed and panicked. Don't do that to yourself.

Some hiring managers will reject you just because you are late. Crazy, huh? But, true.

7.3 **What Will You Wear?**

I'm no fashionista. However, I have some guidelines for you. Do not wear anything to an interview that you would wear to the beach. No flip-flops, no sandals.

Do you need to wear a suit? That depends on the kind of job you're interviewing for. Ask your contact what the acceptable dress code is, if you're concerned. You can always dress more formally than your interviewers. That's not a problem.

At the very least, your clothes should fit, should be clean, and pressed. If you are not sure of this, make a sticky that says something like, "Investigate the state of interview clothing." Put it on your "Ready To Do" column.

You want to wear clothing that presents you in your best light, just as your résumé does.

Does your hair need a trim? Does your deodorant work? Do your teeth need a trip to the dentist? If you are not sure of the answers to these questions, ask a trusted friend.

Ladies, avoid perfume and distracting jewelry. Gentlemen, avoid cologne. Wait until you experience the workplace and see what "normal" is like there.

Brilliant Guy, Horrible Body Odor

I once interviewed a brilliant technical person. He was interviewing in Massachusetts and the rest of the team was in California. Eventually, they would all work together.

They were impressed with his answers. They asked me what I thought.

I agreed. His answers were quite impressive. I also explained that his body odor was as impressive as his answers. Had they checked his references?

No one had. I agreed to check.

Sure enough. You put this guy in a room by himself, he was fine. But in a room with other people? He was impossible. His body odor made it impossible to work with him.

Unless you are brilliant, like this guy, ask for feedback.

You should look and smell neat, clean, and presentable. Pop a breath mint a few minutes before your interview. Yes, your physical appearance counts. It shouldn't, but it does. Look and smell as good as you can.

7.4 Who Is Your First Contact?

You may not know all the people with whom you will interview. The company might change those people at the last minute. However, you do need to know who to ask for, when you arrive. I like to ask for that person's direct line, and maybe their cell. That way, if I encounter traffic or some kind of unforeseeable problem on the road, I can call and explain.

I once had a scheduled call at 2:30 p.m. On the way back from a doctor's appointment, I was less than a mile from my house at 2:00 p.m., and got a flat tire. I was not going to make the call. I called my contact, after calling AAA, and explained the problem. They understood, and we rescheduled the call.

After you arrive, and start the interview, you can ask for the list of people with whom you'll be interviewing. That way, you can send a thank you note after you return home.

7.5 Be Ready to Observe

Part of interviewing is observing what there is to see. For example, do people sit in a cube farm, or do people sit in functional silos, or by project? You can ask. Do you have an opportunity to see where people sit, or do you only see the interviewing location? Where do you interview? I have hair-raising stories of interview locations.

Remember those Questions You Can Ask About Cultural Fit in the Interview, p. 60? You might need to adjust them on the fly. You always want to answer the interviewers' questions first. And, you want to be ready with *your* questions. Interviewing and finding a job is a two-way street. Use your observations to guide you: where people sit, what you see or don't see on the walls.

7.6 Manage the Mundane so You Are Relaxed in the Interview

You might think these are the mundane parts of interview preparation. Maybe they are. They are necessary. If you manage the mundane parts of the interview preparation, you can be relaxed for the interview. You can be the best "you."

Once you've taken care of the interview preparation, you can be ready to answer questions.

7.7 Answer Questions Well

Interviewing candidates and interviewing for a job are two sides of the same coin. When the hiring teams interview candidates, they're looking for data that will help them decide if the candidate can perform the required work here and now. So, they need to know:

- What's the required work?
- How has the candidate performed work like that in the past?
- How can I ask questions so that the candidate can explain their experience?
- When you're the candidate, you have similar objectives:
- What's the required work?
- Have I performed work like that in the past? If not, is there relevant experience I can discuss that is useful to my interviewer?
- How do I explain that work to the interviewer?

Both you and the interviewers have the same goals. So, your job is to tell your interviewers the stories of your work. Not fantasies, but the real stories of what happened. That's called a conversation.

The best interview is a conversation between two people. Not all interviewers realize that. The interviewers who do realize that they will get more from a conversation than stupid games and riddles will ask questions like these:

- **Closed** questions to establish the facts.
- **Open-ended** questions to help you explain your story. **Behavior-description** questions are the best type of open-ended question.
- **Auditions** are a technique that allows the interviewer see you *perform* your work.
- **Meta-questions** are questions about the interview or question. "Is there something else I should be asking you?"

With any luck, your interviewers will plan which kinds of questions to ask about what's important to them. If not, you can help your interviewers interview you.

Some interviewers like *hypothetical* questions. They believe they can perceive how you would behave in a situation if they ask you. I caution interviewers against those kinds of questions, because hypothetically, I'm perfect. Hypothetically, I never make mistakes. In reality, I make plenty. If you are lucky enough to get a hypothetical interviewer, run with it. Just know that your hypothetical interview is not the same as the reality will be.

7.8 Be Prepared for Great Interview Questions

Here are some questions your interviewers may ask of you:

Interviewer's goal: Learn about how you approach problem-solving. Your interviewer might ask these questions:

- Tell me about what you are working on now.
- Tell me how you arrived at that solution. What issues did you encounter?
- Tell me about a time you had trouble.
- Your interviewer might listen for these kinds of answers:
- Your involvement with the project.
- Are you aware of your problems?
- What turns you on about your job.
- How sophisticated you are about your solutions.

I like to ask candidates what they have recently read in their field, to see where their interests have taken them.

I like to ask candidates for an example of their initiative. "Give me an example of your initiative in your most recent position." Sometimes I phrase it this way: "Tell me about a time you didn't have enough information to complete an assignment. What did you do?" Or, "What do you do when faced with inadequate requirements?"

The questions I ask new college grads are:

- What's been the most satisfying or challenging for you?
- What have you learned?
- How have you had to adapt?
- Tell me about a time you saw a problem at work. What did you do?
- What did you learn from projects that required working in teams?

Your interviewers may not ask you these questions. However, you can use these questions to prepare for your interview.

7.9 Be Prepared for Auditions

Auditions are another interview technique that helps the interviewers see how you work. Appropriate auditions include giving you a sample of code or product and asking you to do 15 minutes of work or discuss what you see.

If you are not technical, you might need to facilitate a meeting, or give a presentation. Auditions are a way to see you perform the work you might do in a typical day.

You *want* to perform an audition, because you can demonstrate your skills. Auditions are much better than irrelevant questions.

7.10 Reframe Irrelevant Questions

Unfortunately, there are too many bad interviewers out there who think they should ask you irrelevant questions. If you encounter these questions, consider reframing the question so you can give a better answer:

- *Are you goal-oriented/a technical leader/a self-starter?*

Suggest, "Hmm, how about I tell you about a project where the goals were vague?" or "Let me tell you about a time I was a technical leader." Or, "Here's what I did when I didn't know what to do."

This is a leading question, so it's a bad interview question, but interviewers still ask it.

- *What are your strengths?*

If you've ever worked and received a performance evaluation, say, "I received a performance evaluation on this date, and my boss thought I had these strengths." Or, "Let me tell you about an achievement I'm particularly proud of." If you haven't had an evaluation, you could say, "Well, when I worked with so-and-so, I suggested we do this thing, and it was great." "When I worked on name-the-project, I decided to improve this thing." And then tell the story.

- *What are your weaknesses?*

Try and answer something like this: "I don't really know the context here, yet. Let me tell you about areas in which I've been increasing my skills." Or, "I've been working on my knowledge in these areas."

The strengths and weaknesses questions are *bad* interview questions, but interviewers persist in asking them.

- *Where do you want to be in <1 year, 2 years, 5 years>?*

You can say, "I'm not sure. I'd really like to work for awhile and see where my strengths fit into the organization." Or, you can reframe the question and say, "Hmm, are you asking about my ambition? Let me tell you about the time I decided I wanted to do this thing."

I don't see how you can answer that stupid question. (Okay, JR, tell us how you *really* feel.) On the other hand, these interviewers feel as if they are asking you an insightful question. So, tell them about your ability to learn, or your ambition. And, then send them to me to build their interviewing skills.

- *If you had a magic wand, and three wishes, what would they be?*

Reframe that to problem-solving: "Well, I'm not so sure about magic wands, but when I've seen problems at work, here's what I did."

Another question I despair of ever eliminating. If you get this one, or "What animal do you like?" or "If you were on a desert island, what would you want?" don't answer dogs or cats or Brad Pitt or Angelina Jolie. You can imagine me throwing my hands up in despair. Instead, redirect the answer to how you solved a recent problem, or solved a recent conflict. If you have managed to solve world hunger or world peace, by all means, explain.

- Any game or puzzle. You have my sympathies. *Just do it.* Then offer to perform an audition.

7.11 Reframe Illegal Questions

In the US, you cannot ask these questions of a candidate, unless it somehow directly relates to the job:

- Questions relating to race, color, religion, sex, or national origin
- Height and weight
- Marital status or child care arrangements
- Candidate's age
- Ability to speak English (or other natural language) unless that is a requirement for the job
- Arrest record, unless the company has a policy to not hire felons
- Military service
- Financial status
- Year the candidate graduated from college (because you might derive their age from that question)

If someone asks you if you have children, ask "Are you asking me about my ability to travel or work overtime during a release?"

If they ask if you're healthy say, "Do you mean to come to work and do the job?"

If they ask if you're married, you can use humor, "No, my mother wants me to be though, so should I send her your number so you can both gang up on me?" If you choose *not* to use humor, you can say, "Um, is that relevant to the job? Do you need me to be married?"

When I teach people interviewing, this is how I do it. You can ask other job-seeking colleagues to do this with you.

1. Break into groups of three. Work together so that you create three questions about problem-solving skills and three questions about creative skills that apply to your kind of job.

2. In your groups of three, choose an Interviewer, a Candidate, and an Observer.
   - Interviewer: Choose one of the problem-solving questions and one design skill question. Interview the candidate.
   - Observer, write down what you see. Do not make interpretations. After 10 minutes, stop interviewing.
   - Observer, explain what you saw and heard. Candidate, explain what you saw and heard.
   - Change roles. Choose two new questions. Interview. Debrief in your groups, starting with the Observer, then the Candidate.
   - Change roles. Choose last two questions. Interview. Debrief in your groups, starting with the Observer, then the Candidate.

3. Now, spend 10-15 minutes as a final debrief. Consider the facilitated conversation:
   - What did you notice as a Candidate, Interviewer, Observer?
   - What was challenging in each position? What was exciting?
   - What insights do you have?
   - What one thing will you do as a Candidate moving forward?

If you have a support network, you can practice this at a support group meeting.

7.12 Ask Questions of the Hiring Manager and the Interview Team

In an interview, you have an opportunity to ask questions. Good interviewers will ask, "What questions do you have for me?" Be ready with an answer. Do not let this opportunity go to waste!

What questions do you ask? It depends on where you are in the interview process.

First, ask about culture. As a candidate, these are ideal questions to ask in a first-round interview. You may not be able to come right out and ask about culture, but you can ask these kinds of questions of a manager to learn about culture.

- What's okay to talk about?
- How do you treat people?
- What do you reward?

You can also ask questions from your lists, back when you Create Questions You Can Ask About Cultural Fit in the Interview, p. 60.

1. "Give me an example of some of the most recent times you have promoted from within. What did the people do that made them promotable?" You, as a candidate, listen for perseverance or heroic behavior, or something else.

2. "Do you have team meetings? What happens at them?" And, "Does senior management hold all-hands meetings? What happens there?" I have some very funny stories about when I was a manager and one of my best developers had trouble keeping his mouth shut at all-hands company meetings. He wanted to know how we were going to make money. He thought it was a great question. Management thought he was out to embarrass them. Nope. He did *want* to know how the company would make money. It was *not* okay to talk about that topic.

3. You can ask, especially if the organization professes to be agile, "Tell me about your 'sustainable pace' for the most recent three iterations/releases." Feel free to vary that question, depending on where they are in the current release. "Do you have hardening sprints?" might be a good question. If they are doing release trains, I would ask about how they do on the last couple of iterations of the train.

4. If they are not agile, I would ask about "crunch time." "Tell me about project overtime? Do you have any?" You want to know about how the organization treats the project staff.

5. You and I know how bad multitasking is. I would ask, "Tell me about multitasking. Do you assign people to one project at a time, or are people assigned to multiple projects at a time?" This is a closed question. It allows you to ask other questions about how the organization defines the project portfolio.

When I blogged about this, Andy Lester added these questions:

1. "What do you like best about working here?"
2. "How is your department perceived in the organization? Is there friction between this department and others?"

A reader suggested this question:

1. "How much time do you spend in meetings?"

After reflection, I also like:

1. "How is your project perceived by other projects?"

Lori Howard suggests asking this terrific question:

1. "What results do you need to see in three, six, or nine months from the person you hire in order for you to consider this person a success in this position?"

You want to consider the timeframe for that question, depending on the kind of job you are seeking. Ask everyone with whom you interview and see if they give you the same answer. It shows you care about results and that you want to be successful.

In the same vein of asking team members, you might ask these questions to see what you can discuss, how people are treated, and what's rewarded:

1. "How often do you work closely with someone else?" (You want to establish that there is a pattern of close working relationships on the team.)
2. "When you work closely with someone else, how do you bat around ideas, how do you get feedback?" (Those might be

two questions. Ask if there are architects and what the other person's position is.)

3. "If you have a suggestion for improvement, how and when do you raise it?"
4. "What was the best recognition you ever received?"

Even if your interviewer doesn't ask you if you have questions, make sure you do. Use your interviewing time to ask questions. Remember, interviewing is a two-way street. Don't let that time go to waste. Ask about cultural fit.

7.13 Why Are You Leaving Your Current Position?

People leave jobs for many reasons. Maybe you were laid off. Maybe you just graduated from college. Maybe you are leaving because you've learned everything you can, and it's time to move on. Maybe the company has changed location and your commute no longer fits. All of these are looking-forward reasons, and you can say exactly that when people ask you. No problem.

Sometimes people leave jobs because the job they have is the job from hell. If you have a toxic job, do not say so, for any reason.

Whatever the reason, make sure you *know* your reason. Because your interviewer will ask.

 Never criticize a present or past company. Never. Bite your tongue first.

Prepare an answer to this question, so you can answer it as if you are a mature, sensible individual, even if you don't feel as if you are a mature, sensible person. At some point in your life, especially if you find a new job, you will look back on this time and have a mature perspective on this job. I promise you.

You can say things such as, "It's not a good cultural fit for me," as long as you stop there. If the interviewer persists and asks what is not a good fit, you need to have one or two examples. Take a project or one example of not very good management behavior.

If you have had many weeks and weekends of project overtime, you can say, "We are not being successful as a project. I am all for small pushes when we need it. But we are supposed to be agile, and we have nothing like sustainable pace. I'm trying not to complain here, but I'm really concerned about what will happen when we get to what will be the final demo in three months. We are not running this project like an agile project. I've tried to suggest things and every time I've tried to suggest changes, I get shut down. So, I've decided to look for a place that *wants* improvements."

Or, if you have a toxic manager, you could say, "When we are in the middle of discussing a problem as a team, and my manager comes in the room and starts to scream at us to make us solve problems faster, I don't work well under those conditions. So I've decided to look for a place where the managers don't yell at people when we try to fix problems."

You must not blame people for being people, or blame the situation. You do not want to burn bridges. On the other hand, you do want to make it clear that you do not want that particular situation again.

Instead, explain what you are moving *towards*. Do you want a different role? Different responsibility? Do you want to make a different contribution?

If you have learned all you can, and there is no place for you to grow, you can say, "I learned all I could. I advanced as far as I could. I'm looking for new challenges. My manager is a reference." *Well, assuming your manager is a reference.*

And, if your company has relocated, say, "I enjoyed my time with the company. But when they moved and my commute grew, it became clear it was time for me to leave."

Think about your Career Line, p. 55 and the circumstances that brought you the most satisfaction. And, remember your Questions You Can Ask About Cultural Fit in the Interview, p. 60. Unless you're a recent grad, you have plenty of positive ways to answer this question.

7.14 Bad Questions Interviewers Love to Ask

These questions are bad because they don't have enough context for the candidate. I don't find much value in these questions, but other interviewers love to ask them. So, be ready for them. They are:

- Why should I hire you?
- Why do you want to work here?
- Why will you fit here?...or some other version of this question
- What do you like to do?

We'll take them one at a time.

7.14.1 *Why should I hire you?*

When you answer this, be specific. Make sure you've researched the company and the position during the interview. If the first interviewer asks this question, you might says something like this: "From what I read in the ad/job description, it sounds like my experience in this job," and I would point to that job on my résumé and then provide the interviewer with specific examples of my experience. Give a behavior-description example. If you can, provide a couple of examples.

7.14.2 *Why do you want to work here?*

You want to sound as if you look forward to this job. Interviewers can *smell* people running away from current jobs. They want to know you are looking forward to their job, not just grasping at any job or running away from a job. This is where cultural fit matters. Have you looked at the corporate mission and compared it to yours? Do the products make a difference to you? How about the people—do you know any of them? You need something to latch onto and make it your own. This is why spraying résumés doesn't work.

7.14.3 *How will you fit here?*

Some interviewers even ask, "Why would you be a perfect fit?" But you might get a question such as, "Tell me how you started on your most recent project," which is a much better question. Now you have a chance to discuss how you integrated yourself onto a team. And that's how you want to answer this question. How do you start working with people when you join a new team?

7.14.4 *What do you like to do?*

Some interviewers think this is a great open-ended question. It is open-ended. However, it is a terrible question, because it has no context.

You can turn this question around, and say, "The most recent time I was a whatever-the-job-is, I was able to do . . ." and then tell a terrific story of one of your successes. You can use a behavior-description answer to a bad question.

Interviewers will never stop asking bad questions. If you have prepared a résumé that represents your value and have the stories of your career, you are ready.

If you want to read more about interviewing from the perspective of the hiring manager or team, read *Hiring Geeks That Fit* (ROT12).

7.15 Be Ready to Answer: What Have You Done Since . . .

Many interviewers like to ask the question, "What have you done since your last job?" especially if they see you are unemployed. In fact, they will ask this question if they see a break on your résumé for any reason at all.

If you've been sitting around eating bonbons, this is not a good question for you. On the other hand, let's assume you've accomplished many things in your break between jobs, or in your break between graduating and finding a job. Maybe you have:

- Volunteered, to build your professional skills. If you're technical, maybe you participated in an open-source project. Add that to your résumé.

- Volunteered in your community to build your network.
- Enrolled in classes to build or refresh your skills.
- Read a number of professional books. This one counts.

If you are unemployed, make sure you are not sitting around, feeling sorry for yourself. You will sound desperate. Hiring managers can perceive that and be reluctant to bring you in for an interview. Do something.

7.16 Write a Thank-You Note

I suggest you write a thank-you note, if you liked the job and want to maintain the conversation. You don't have to. It's a nice touch, and one that will help people remember you.

It can be a quick email, such as this to the hiring manager:

Hi so-and-so,

I really enjoyed my interview with you and the entire team today.

As I said in the interview, my skills in collaboration and data structures would fit your needs well. I hope we continue to move forward.

Sincerely,

Joan Candidate

That's it. You don't need to say more. You don't need to handwrite the note either. Snail-mail takes too long. Email is fine.

7.17 Now Do This

1. Prepare a few interview questions and answers, especially about some areas you think might be your weakness. Maybe you are concerned about gaps in your employment history. Maybe you have other concerns. Now is the time to practice, preferably with others.

2. Prepare your questions for the hiring manager and the hiring team members.

3. Practice interviewing so you are prepared.

CHAPTER 8
Decide How You Will Decide on an Offer

At some point, you will receive an offer. Congratulations! Now you have to decide what to do. How will you decide?

 Beware of deciding solely on salary. If you do, you run the risk of repeating your dissatisfactory job patterns. Why? Because you have not thought of what you need for your mastery, autonomy, or purpose (PIN09).

Use the Career Analysis you did in Know Your Previous Job Patterns, p. 53 to help you answer the following questions:

Is this the job you want? Did you look for a company, maybe when you asked for an Informational Interview, p. 107, and you made a warm connection with someone, applied for a job, and they liked you and made you an offer? You have to decide:

1. Is this the right offer for me?
2. Is this the right level of job?
3. Do the salary and all of the other perks, fit for me?

You need to know yourself. With any luck, you have already read and practiced the job timeline exercise in Know Your Previous Job Patterns, p. 53. If not, do that now.

 If you are unemployed and have been for a while, you might be saying, "I'm taking this job. Period." That's fine. Sometimes the risk of *not* taking the first job you are offered is greater than the risk of even assessing the offer. Read this section for the future.

What would make this job high in satisfaction for you? Is it near the center of the city, so you can go to the theater after work? Is it near hiking trails, so you can take a walk every day after lunch? Is it a two-mile commute from home? Or, do you prefer a longer drive, so you can listen to books on tape?

Do you see how none of us has the same criteria for satisfaction? I don't know what a high satisfaction job means for you. This is why your Career Analysis is so critical for you.

8.1 Is This Job Right for Me?

There are several parts to the question, "Is this job right for me?" You work for a company, a manager, and with a team. Depending on the type of job, those different parts will matter more or less. The manager part always matters a lot, because your relationship with your manager is the biggest factor in whether you will enjoy your job or be miserable in your job (BUC99).

The company has a culture, also. Your manager puts his or her own stamp on that culture, which is why I suggested you do the exercise in Know Your Previous Job Patterns. Some managers influence the corporate culture more than others. You will be able to work for some managers and not for others—regardless of the corporate culture.

8.2 Is This the Right Job Level?

If you have been a technical lead and you are searching for a management job, what do you do if you receive an offer for a technical lead job? This is where you might reflect on your networking, interviewing, LinkedIn profile, everything to do with your job search. You might be presenting yourself as a technical lead. You might not be *ready* for a management job. You might not *want* a management job. You might ask for feedback.

But, if you want a management job, and you think you have done everything in your power to obtain a management job, you can problem solve and negotiate with the hiring manager. You do not have to take the job *at this level*. If you thought the job was a management job, you can ask, "I thought when I applied for this job, it was a management job. Was I mistaken?"

You need feedback to understand what the hiring manager is thinking. Ask for it.

If the hiring manager does not think you can do the job at the higher level, well, better you should discover that now. If you have a job, work at the higher level, rewrite your résumé so people can see your accomplishments, and continue. Or, consider taking the offer and ask for a review in the future. Or, decide to apply elsewhere.

If you see this in your search continually, you might not be networking with people at the right level. If you want a director position, you need to network with VPs and directors. Why? VPs hire directors. Directors might know when peer positions are available.

 There are fewer management positions in any industry. That doesn't mean you shouldn't search for one. Be aware your chances of landing one recede and you are competing with more people.

Remember, the more specific your desired management position, the fewer of them there are. You will need to search longer. You might have to expand the geography of your search, the product domain, and possibly your salary expectations to get the title.

8.3 Does the Offer Fit What I Want?

Many of us think of salary as the primary driver of an offer. It is. But job offers can be much more than salary.

Salary is the starting point in the negotiation for any job offer. Maybe you want tuition reimbursement. Or a conference budget. Or a book budget. Or something else. Maybe you need more in the area of autonomy, such as more vacation time (paid or unpaid, depending on your seniority) or purpose. Remember than when it comes to an offer, *everything* is negotiable. Everything.

First, you need to know your job patterns. Since I am motivated by mastery and autonomy (remember my values are about learning and control), I want things such as the above. But you might not.

I wrote a post about this on my blog, What to Offer in Addition to Salary[1]. What you will want depends on your motivation (PIN09), and how much of your personal motivation is autonomy, mastery, or purpose.

Maybe you are looking for a job in a particular industry, which will fulfill your need for purpose. In that case, maybe you can address the components of autonomy and mastery in the offer. Maybe you fulfill the purpose part of your motivation outside of work.

 There is no such thing as work life balance. There is only life. Live it.

Remember that you only have one life. There is no such thing as work life balance. You need to be happy in a job. If you can't make the offer fit what you want, should you take it?

I can't tell you *not* to take an offer. I *can* tell you to prepare for the negotiation and to generate more options, so you are ready for the negotiation.

8.4 Prepare for Your Negotiation

You have to be ready before you start negotiating. Sometime in your first few weeks of your job search, you want to answer these questions for yourself:

- What do I want as a minimum salary?
- What do I want in addition to that minimum salary?

These are your negotiation points.

---

[1]http://www.jrothman.com/blog/htp/2011/02/what-to-offer-in-addition-to-salary.html

Now, for every open position you are seriously interested in, you can ask yourself:

- What is the job worth to the company?
- How easy is it for the company to fill the position?
- What is the job worth to you?
- Is it worth it to me to take a lower or different title to take this job?
- How easy is it for you to find a new job? You want to assess the tradeoffs of continuing to look versus taking this offer.

8.5 Generate Multiple Options For Yourself

One of the best things you can do while deciding on an offer is to generate multiple options (HEA13). It's best if you have multiple offers. Sometimes, you only have one offer.

Remember the Rule of Three for Generating More Ideas, p. 139: one option is a trap, two is a dilemma, three options starts to provide you real choices and breaks your logjam thinking. Whatever you do, generate at least three options every time you have an offer.

If you only have one offer, you always have the option to take that offer or reject it. But maybe you have these options as well:

- Negotiate for something that's not currently in the offer that would make the offer more attractive.
- Nudge a hiring manager into moving faster once you have an offer in hand. Maybe you can see two offers.
- Network with other people who have worked or are working at this company to see what they think about this company.
- Offer to work as a temporary employee for 90 days, to see if you both like you in this job.

Sometimes, it's easy to make a decision about a potential job. Sometimes it's not. You might try a list of pros and cons if you are stuck. You may want to think things through first and then talk to someone. You might want to talk things out with a friend or a colleague. If you have a networking group, maybe use one of your colleagues there. You might want to think about, "What would happen if I took this job?" and "What would happen if I don't take this job?"

If you need more guidance about how to expand your decision-making choices, *Decisive: How to Make Better Choices in Life and Work* (HEA13) is an excellent read.

You always have more options than "Do I take this job or not?"

8.6 Now Do This

1. Know what you want in an offer, before you start interviewing. What is your minimum salary?
2. Do you have anything else that you want in addition to salary?
3. What are your tradeoffs? What are the tradeoffs for the company?

PART III

Build Your Network

I wrote this section specifically with shy people in mind. Think of these networking tips as a menu, not as something you need to follow in a straight line.

Help potential employers find you.

CHAPTER 9

Network, Network, Network

In real estate, the mantra is "location, location, location." When you look for a job, the mantra is "network, network, network."

How will potential hiring managers find you? You have to be at the top of their minds. That means you need to have networked with them *before* they know they need you. You want to do background networking all the time. In addition, you need to have a targeted marketing plan, p. 108, so you can target the kinds of organizations that you think you will be happy at. If you have a Target Marketing Plan, p. 108, you can avoid the spray-and-pray approach to résumés.

Which kinds of networking do you do first? It depends on what you are comfortable with. If you are not comfortable networking at all, if you haven't paid attention to your network, start with background networking, and build your self-confidence for one to three weeks.

9.1 Start Background Networking Immediately

If you have not been paying attention to your network, that's okay. Start here. Even if you *have* been paying attention to your network, start here.

9.2 Use Your Alumni Networks

You have alumni networks in a variety of places. You have the schools you attended: high school, undergraduate, and graduate school; the clubs you joined; the companies at which you held intern positions; the companies at which you held part-time positions; and the companies you worked at before you started looking for this position. All of those places are potential alumni networks.

Your undergraduate and graduate schools and your previous companies are the best sources of potential alumni networks. However, if you are a recent grad, don't discount the clubs, especially if you held a leadership position. People who graduated a year or two ahead of you might remember you, and will be ready to lend a helping hand. That's the point of the alumni network.

9.3 Join the List or Group

First, you must find and join the alumni email list or group.

I cannot emphasize this point enough. Your school or work alumni email list does you no good if you do not join it. If you attended the school for at least two years, join the list. If your school alumni are uptight and really want to know that you graduated, fine. But if you were really close to graduating, or you should have graduated, ask to join the list. Chances are good they will let you. The list does you no good if you don't join it.

If you worked for a company that was a pioneer in its field, or a cool startup, or was large, or was small, or if the people who worked there shared some significant history, someone has created a mailing list. From that mailing list, someone started a LinkedIn group. Find it and get on that group.

Some of you, especially if you are on the shy side, might be worried about joining lists or groups. Joining the group doesn't make you a "joiner" or an extrovert; it makes you a smart networker.

You need an "in" with people, and joining the group provides you a warmer introduction. So join the group and don't complain. I'm not asking you to call anyone. I'm asking you to send a request on LinkedIn and ask to join the group with evidence that should be in your profile.

Join the group. You can't network with these people if you don't join the group.

9.4 Use the List

Once you've joined the group, monitor the list for people looking for work, for open positions, and for people asking for help.

Whatever you do, do not involve this group in any multi-level marketing programs. Well, don't do that if you want to get hired. The people on the group will remember. And their memories will not be kind to you.

Since you are looking for work, you want to increase the number of first-degree connections you have. The more first-level connections you have on LinkedIn, and the more active you are on LinkedIn, the more likely you are to be noticed. LinkedIn will send your name out every week with your new activity to your first-level network names, which helps increase your network activity. "Oh, Johanna connected with five more people last week. I wonder who those people were." That activity leads people to think of you when it comes to networking.

You also want to establish yourself as a helpful person. The more you offer help, the more questions you answer on LinkedIn, the more people will think of you, which will increase your reputation. This is a Good Thing.

So, how do you do this without being obnoxious? You ask people with whom you worked closely first to connect with you. And, as you help people on the group who are looking for work, or help people who have questions, you connect with them.

Networking is not a fast activity, like making a cup of coffee. You nurture your network, and grow it. Spend time on your network every week. Decide how much time to spend in each group each week.

You may decide that you want to spend a total timebox of one hour on LinkedIn for a given week. Maybe that week you spend time on one school group and one ex-company group, and that's it. Or, maybe you spend time on two ex-company lists, and that's it. Or, you spend time on two professional groups, because that's where you think your time is best spent that week. And that's it.

If you provide value in other ways, such as blogging articles of interest to the group, you can post those articles as points of discussion for the group. You want to *give* to the group. Make sure the articles are relevant to the group.

9.5 Remember Your Etiquette

Remember that the people you network with are doing you a favor. Be nice to them. Treat them as if their time is valuable. It is. That's why you want to remember your etiquette when you network in your alumni groups:

- Explain your qualifications in two to three sentences. Do not list everything that is so wonderful about you.
- Offer to link directly with anyone in the group. After all, you are all in the group!
- Thank people in the group in advance for their help.
- If someone helps you specifically, thank that person in the group and more specifically off-group.
- Make sure you have a smiling picture in your LinkedIn profile. If you don't, you are unlikely to get help.

Your alumni networks may not pay off immediately. But your contributions might make a few more people think of you first, which is exactly what you want.

Since you are an alum, people may remember you and provide you feedback on your LinkedIn profile. Listen to the feedback. You decide what to do with the feedback. But listen carefully. Maybe ask a few more people what they think.

9.6 Network With People Who Are Loose Connections

Here's something that might surprise you. The best networking connections for you are looser, rather than tighter (PFE10). If you already know people well, you know the jobs they have to offer. They know who the candidates are.

If you really want to find a new job, you need to exploit your connections in ways you haven't exploited them before. I mean exploit in the sense of "make the best use of." That means that you want to network with your friends. And, you want to network with your children's friends or your parents' friends, depending on how old you are.

This is why it's so important to use all of your alumni networks on LinkedIn.

Do you belong to a religious institution, country club, or other personal or professional society you have not yet mined for contacts? Network with those people. Add them to your LinkedIn network.

9.7 Network at Professional Society Meetings

Another way to build loose connections is to build connections through professional interests. You can and should network online by joining professional groups on LinkedIn.

And, that's not enough. Because it's difficult to build rapport online. It's much easier to build rapport in person. If you live in a place where there are professional society meetings, plan to attend one or two every month. Once you've met some of these people in person, they are much more likely to accept your invitation to connect.

These meetings can feel intimidating to you if you are shy or an introvert. So, find a buddy and go together. Now you have someone to talk to, no matter what.

9.8 Ask for Recommendations

I bet your résumé says, "References upon request." That's fine, but it's not enough. Of course you can provide references upon request. And, wouldn't it be nice if you had a couple of recommendations on LinkedIn, just so people could see how great you are?

You can ask people for recommendations on LinkedIn. In fact, you should. Consider asking some of these people during your first few weeks of job-hunting:

- One of your college advisors if you are a recent grad
- A recent manager
- A couple of colleagues with whom you recently worked
- People with whom you have worked on volunteer or open-source projects

You can initiate the recommendations by writing a recommendation for these people. They are more likely to provide a recommendation for you if you write one for them first.

If you don't feel comfortable writing a recommendation, for, say a college advisor, but you do feel comfortable asking for one, you have several alternatives for asking for a recommendation.

 Provide recommendations first. Then ask for one.

You can initiate a general email conversation outside of a LinkedIn mail if you've been out of touch for awhile. Explain that you are reconnecting and you are looking for recommendations and networking. Then once you've exchanged pleasantries, and you've connected on LinkedIn, send a direct LinkedIn mail requesting a recommendation. LinkedIn has a specific recommendation request form that you do not have to personalize.

The second alternative if you've already connected with people is to use that specific LinkedIn recommendation request form and customize the language. In this alternative, you are not connecting with people for the first time and requesting a recommendation, you are requesting the recommendation on the basis of your already-existing relationship. You might need to jog your colleague's memory: "Two years ago, when you were my advisor in my senior year, we discussed so-and-so. Well, I've been working doing such-and-such, and it's been great. I'm now looking for a new job doing this-and-that and I'd like your recommendation so potential employers can see I was thinking about it in my senior year of college."

Ask people with whom you have a close working relationship, even if that relationship is of short duration. If they have seen you work and can vouch for you, their recommendation is valid. Do not ask people who have not seen you work. Their recommendation is useless.

Caution: Do NOT ask your friends to write recommendations for you, unless you have worked together, and there is a basis for the recommendation. Instead, as you gain more friends who have worked in the industry, ask if they can *refer* you to their friends or companies. One of the best jobs I had was because a friend referred me. Sure, I had built my technical skills, but his referral made a huge difference.

9.9 Ask for Informational Interviews

Is there a company that sounds like a perfect fit for you? You look at the website, and what the site says looks great. The corporate mission looks like something you would say. The company even has a job that sort of, kind of, looks like something you could do.

Before you apply, look to see if you know someone who works there. Or, even someone who knows someone. You will be better off if you can apply via their employee referral program or from an informational interview than from an application through their website.

When you use LinkedIn to ask for an informational interview, you can craft a *short* introduction that looks like a cover letter and says something like this:

Dear so-and-so,

I hope you are doing well. (Feel free to customize this even more. Do not refer to the drunken bash over New Year's.)

I see you are connected to Susie Project Manager at MyDesiredCo. Are you willing to provide me a brief introduction to her? I would like a 15-minute informational phone call about my-desired-position.

Insert a brief sentence about why you would be great for this job. Maybe something like this: As a business analyst, I'm fascinated by the emphasis her project places on interviewing customers to hone their requirements. I've done that before and gotten great results.

It looks as if MyDesiredCo my-desired-position does similar activities, so I'd like to get Susie's feedback about whether I would be a good match for the open my-desired-position.

Thanks, YourName

I can't guarantee you will get the interview, but now you have a warm introduction, not just a cold application.

9.10 Join a Networking Support Group

One of the best things you can do for yourself is to join a networking support group. The best ones are free. In the Boston area, I'm familiar with WIND, Wednesday is Networking Day[1]. They meet once a week. The meetings provide you with a structure for your job search, and help you network with other people. Others will encounter jobs that are not good for them, but might be good for you.

9.11 Develop Your Target Marketing Plan

You might decide to develop your targeted marketing plan first, rather than your background networking. If your résumé is ready, and you don't need any support, go right ahead. Some people need a few weeks of practice with networking before they develop their marketing plan.

If you have defined your purpose, back in Define Your Purpose, p. 64, you can define what you will say about yourself to a hiring manager at a target company. You will have a brief explanation of what you can do for that manager. If you have articulated your value on your résumé, you can provide evidence you can perform the work for that manager.

---

[1]http://www.windnetworking.net/

It sounds easy, doesn't it? It requires a plan.

9.12 Plan to Market Yourself

You are marketing yourself. Are you surprised? Don't be. You have articulated your value on your résumé. I hope you've taken the time to define your purpose. Now, you need to match your purpose and value with potential employers. You are explaining how valuable you are. That's marketing.

There's a great book by Orville Pierson that describes how to do this in detail. It's called *The Unwritten Rules of the Highly Effective Job Search* (PIE06).

Your plan has these components:

1. Decide on the work you want to do. You already did that, when you reviewed your job patterns, wrote your résumé, and articulated your value.
2. Now you are thinking about the organizations you want to work for. Who will you put on your list of companies? Maybe you have potential managers you want to work for?
3. Decide on the message you want to tell them. If you have already defined your purpose, make sure your purpose is congruent with the targeted companies' mission.

9.13 Create a List of Target Companies or Target Managers

How do you create a your target list? If you've been networking all along, you have people in your network at companies who do work that is similar to what you want to do. Or, they know people who do work that is similar. You put those people on your list.

Do those people need to be hiring managers? It's nice if they are. They don't need to be. They need to be people who can introduce you to hiring managers.

Remember, the best networking is with loose connections. This is why building your background network, even before you build your target list is so important. You haven't asked for anything when you reconnected with people. You extended a friendly hand. You told people you were looking. Now, if you say to someone in your network, "I realize that your company is a place I'd like to work," that person has a warm feeling. You've already built rapport with the first connection. Now, you've improved on the first connection.

9.14 Decide on Your Message

When you contact people on your target list, you need a specific message.

If you decided on your purpose, back in Define Your Purpose, p. 64, you can use that to refine your message. You do want to say you are looking for a job. In addition, you want to mention something about your purpose. Here are some examples of messages I've heard:

> I'm looking for a job as an embedded systems programmer in an agile organization. I've done that for the last three years, and we released three products on time and our customers were really happy. I'm interested in your company because of your Product A. —Developer writing to a Hiring Manager

> I'm looking for a job as an agile project manager. That fits with my experience on geographically distributed agile teams. I'm interested in organizations such as (large organizations 1, 2, 3). —Project manager in a networking environment

> I'm looking for a job, moving up as a senior manager in a technical organization. I've done everything else, and now it's time to move up. I've been working with some startups for the last couple of years, and I'm now interested in looking at organizations such as (medium size organizations 1, 2, 3). — Technical leader, looking for a higher level position

When you provide example organizations, try to provide three examples. Our minds are wired to expect three examples. If you only provide one or two examples, your listener will only hear those examples, and won't think of you for other similar organizations. Once your listener hears three examples, your listener will take the examples and make the generalization to a larger list.

Can you just say "I'm looking for a job?" Yes. That's a weak introduction. No one will remember you. But you can say it. In these previous examples, people will remember why you are looking for a job, and you have an excuse for a more inviting conversation.

You can use this message in email or in an in-person networking conversation.

9.15 Put Your Target List on Your ToDo List

As you create your ToDo list each week, check to see that you are somehow approaching someone on your target list every week. That way, you know that your networking has focus.

If you network without focus, you'll add people to your network, but you won't be getting closer to finding a job. You want to network with focus.

9.16 Network with Focus

I said you want to do "background network" activities, such as online networking and professional group networking. I even have a chapter on how to Use Social Media to Network, p. 113. But if all you ever do is these background networking activities, without thinking of the specific companies or hiring managers, you will discover that your job search will take much longer.

Focus your networking on companies that you want to work for. How? By looking at your values and what success means for you.

You Defined What Success Looks Like For You, p. 65, and you learned about your values from What Did You Learn From Your Career Line, p. 57. If you start to investigate successful companies in the area in which you want to work, and review their mission statements, you will see if your values intersect. See if what you define as success might be what they define as success. If you have intersection, put that company on your target list.

This could take you a while. You might want to use online job boards as a source to investigate companies. Companies looking for people are a good start.

9.17 Can't I Just Apply for Open Positions?

Sure. You can. You can be one of the many minions who apply.

You will have a better chance of getting the job if an employee refers you. Or, if the hiring manager knows you. That's what you get when you do targeted networking.

Does targeted networking take more of your time? Of course it does. Do you have to think more? Sure.

This kind of networking is focused. You will spend time deciding where to spend your time, and you will focus your time. You already decided that "spray-and-pray" didn't work for your résumé, right? It's the same for your networking, too.

If you go to the same old meetings, and meet the same old people, you will get the same old results. You need to make sure you network with focus, and target the companies or hiring managers who will actually hire you.

It takes more work. It's worth it. You have a system, personal kanban, which will allow you to see your progress every week.

9.18 Now Do This

1. List all the ways you have used your network in the past week. Is your network working for you? If not, what do you have to do to improve it?
2. Did you make a list of target companies? What would it take for you to make a list of target companies?
3. Are you meeting anyone for informational interviews? If not, why not?

CHAPTER 10

Use Social Media to Network

It's a brave new world. If you are not using social media, you are not taking advantage of many of the job opportunities available to you.

10.1 How to Get into LinkedIn

You may not be on LinkedIn right now. You've noticed that I consider LinkedIn the cornerstone of a reasonable job search at this time. If you don't want to use LinkedIn, okay. Your search will be *much* more difficult.

If you are not on LinkedIn, go to http://www.linkedin.com[1] and join. You have to sign up with your name, email address, and password. If you are not on LinkedIn, do it now. Right now. I'll wait. Go ahead. Now, wasn't that easy?

10.2 Do I Have to Build My LinkedIn Network?

Some of you are reading this and the networking chapters thinking, "Johanna wants me to be an outgoing personality, collecting people. That's just not me. I don't want to do that."

You need to stay true to yourself. I do not want you to become me. That would be horrible.

Here is the stark reality of job searching in the 21st century: you need a network to find a good job that will match your cultural preferences.

You either need a network to find a recruiter who can help you, or you need a network to find someone who can help introduce you via

---

[1]http://www.linkedin.com

an employee referral, or you need a network to find a job via LinkedIn or Twitter. That's the reality now. The reality might change in a few years. If you don't maintain and build your network, you will not be able to find your next job.

If you work in a very large organization, other people in that organization check LinkedIn to see what you have done to see if they want you on their project. Why? Because the information inside their organization is stale. If you work in a medium-size organization or a small organization, you don't bring just your experience with you, you bring your contacts with you. Your contacts are valuable.

So, be picky about who you choose as contacts. Be selective about how many people you connect with and when. Choose your groups with care. Decide how you will participate. Maybe you don't want to add even three people a week to your network, although I think that's a mistake.

It's not my job search: it's yours. That's why you have a reflection every week, to ask yourself if you are happy about the choices you made. If you are, fine. You don't answer to me. You answer to yourself.

You owe it to yourself to build your connections on LinkedIn. You owe it to yourself to follow people on Twitter. And, even though I don't recommend that you use FaceBook for networking for a job, if you do choose to network on FaceBook, you owe it to yourself to increase your friends on FaceBook.

You owe it to yourself to connect with people and network. This is your life we're talking about here.

10.3 Use Twitter to Network

If you are looking for a job, you can't ignore Twitter. It's a great source of job leads. You don't need to have a Twitter id; you can search through without one. But, you do need to know how to search Twitter.

10.4 Learn to Love Hashtags

Hashtags are your friend. Go to Twitter.com. In the search box, enter #job or #jobsearch or #job #search. You will see the results of your search with those keywords.

If you want to see a real-time stream of potential hashtags, use a tool such as hootsuite.com[2], create an id, and start with job or job search. I will tell you that I wrote this part of the book a couple of times, so things change. Be ready to adapt your tool selection or your search mechanism.

You will see what everyone is saying on Twitter. And, you will also see gems, such as when Susan Joyce, also known as [@JobHuntOrg] tweets about resources to help you with your job search or open jobs.

10.5 Hone Your Search Skills

When you search on hashtags, such as #programmer or #security, you might not find anything. If you remove the #, you might find something different.

Say you are a linguist looking for a job. Anywhere. You have experience in Middle Eastern and Asian languages. Here's how I would search: #jobsearch #linguist.

That returned one potential job the day I looked, in Farsi. But, you don't have experience in Farsi. So, it's time to try another search: #linguist #job. That search returned 12 tweets in the last 24 hours, and another 6 tweets from the previous week.

Now, that's not a lot of tweets, but each one of those is a lead. Each one of those is a person or an organization you can introduce yourself to via the networking I discussed earlier. You look at that person's tweets, web page, LinkedIn page. You might consider introducing yourself.

If you are looking for a finance job, you search for finance. If you are searching for a nanny job, you search #nanny #job. But what if you

---

[2]http://www.hootsuite.com/

have a BA in philosophy and you don't know what you want to do? Or, what if you could do any number of things?

You have these choices:

- Search for several potential jobs simultaneously, depending on your targeted lists. How many companies or jobs are on your target lists? If there are many, maybe you choose one to focus on for now. If there are not too many, or they don't pay enough for you, maybe you keep your options open for now.
- Consider going back to the Define Your Purpose, p. 64 section.
- Invest some time with a career coach.

You have to decide on one ToDo at a time. You have to start a search. That's why you have your board with your ToDos. Make your list of ToDos, one sticky for each ToDo. Now you have your list. Make one of your search ToDos your #1 ToDo. Now you can start. Doesn't that feel better?

10.6 How to Start a Twitter Search

What if you're a new grad or you're new to the job search market after a long time away or you're making a big career shift? What then?

Maybe you know where you want to live. If so, find the hashtag for jobs near where you live. That will lead you to people with jobs in your area. Now you can search those jobs and see if you might like any of them. For example, I live in the Boston area. I would use a search such as #Boston #job.

Maybe you know the industry you want to work in, such as #pharma or #healthcare. You can search on those hashtags, plus your location, or those hashtags, plus #jobsearch.

Start somewhere and follow the links. You can't search for a job on Twitter unless you start.

10.7 Join the Twitterverse

I did say before you don't need a Twitter id. But, I do recommend you don't just watch Twitter, you participate.

When you are ready to join the Twitterverse, you can build your reputation and show potential employers you are *more* than your résumé. The *Twitter Job Search Guide: Find a Job and Advance Your Career in Just 15 Minutes a Day* (WHI10) recommends you tweet your cover letter and/or résumé. That might not fit for you. It would not fit for me. But I do think you can use Twitter to make friends and network in a way that is different from networking in person.

If you are going to search on Twitter—and you should—why not join Twitter? You don't have to tweet much. You can read more than you write.

Think about being helpful. If you are helpful on Twitter, that might be good for building your reputation.

When you join Twitter, make sure you have a professional sounding twitter id, that your profile looks professional, and that you have a picture.

10.7.1 *Do You Have a Picture Yet?*

Okay, here I go again with the picture. People are more apt to follow you and link with you if they see a smiling picture of you. Why? Because this is *social* media.

Remember, you can iterate on your picture just as you iterate on your résumé.

10.8 Follow People Who Have Useful Information and Jobs

If you do nothing else, find the people you *must* follow on Twitter. Once you start searching, you will see people who post useful information every day. Look for people who have jobs that appear to be similar to ones you might want. Those people might be recruiters. They might be hiring managers.

Don't assume you will find the right job your first time searching Twitter. Remember at the beginning of this chapter I talked about location? Searching for a job on Twitter is a lot like searching for a house or an apartment when you don't know where you want to live. You're getting a feel for what's out there.

Social media networking is like asking your friends which neighborhoods are good. Networking is putting out the feelers, time and time again. Keep looking.

Keep following the people on Twitter (and on LinkedIn) who might be the right people. You can't tell if they are the right people unless you follow them.

Follow their tweets. Read their blogs. Look for their information. What's the worst thing that could happen? You waste a few minutes of your time reading. A good thing that could happen is you find a lead. The best thing that could happen is you find a job.

Two caveats:

1. Twitter changes all the time. This is a starting guide to Twitter. You, the jobseeker, will have to keep your information current and keep searching.
2. Consider timeboxing the amount of time you spend on social media. Twitter and all internet-related searching can eat your entire day away. You might want to use a timer so you can plan your time.

10.9 Now Do This

1. How have you expanded your network, both in-person and online, since you started reading this book?
2. Are you on LinkedIn? Have you connected with me and explained that you bought this book so I will know to connect with you? Do you have a picture on LinkedIn and Twitter?
3. Have you asked for any informational interviews?

Now comes the hard part. Everyone needs different tips, and everyone falls into different traps. Depending on your age and experience, decide which of the tips and traps in the next section apply to you.

PART IV

Iterate Through These Job Hunting Traps and Tips

CHAPTER 11

Avoid These Traps

Using timeboxes and personal kanban as a project management approach helps us avoid traps. Even so, it helps to articulate the traps, so we can see how to avoid them.

11.1 Be Kind to Yourself; Don't Beat Yourself Up

After you send an email or make a phone call or have an interview, you might replay your actions and say to yourself, "Oh, I could have written that cover email better, or answered that question better, or asked that question better, or done something different." Fine.

Can you do anything about this with this prospective employer now? If so, act. Can you do anything differently the rest of this week that will make a difference for your job search right now? Make a sticky and put it on your list of ToDos.

If your thoughts are not going to help you right now, this week, write yourself a card or a sticky and put it in your Parking Lot, p. 18 so you can evaluate everything in your Parking Lot during your retrospective. Now, forget about it until your retrospective.

Dwelling on it will not help your self-esteem and will prevent you from making progress. You have written it down, so you can address it. Now, forget it. Stressing about it further only reduces your self-esteem. That doesn't help you find a job.

11.2 Perfection Rules Trap Us Every Time

One of the common mistakes we all make is to seek perfection. One of the ways timeboxing can help you is to allow you to finish something good enough for now, and add a task to your ToDo list to make it better later.

Do not seek perfection in anything so that it paralyzes you. I met a colleague who did not have a photo on her LinkedIn profile. She's been out of work for several months. What's preventing her from adding her picture? She's a better photographer than her friends, but her hardware is not working. What will get her hardware working? A new disk drive. When will she get a new disk drive? In a few more weeks.

How long has she been missing a photo on her profile? The entire time she's been looking for a job. Instead of waiting for a perfect picture, she would be better off with a reasonable picture that shows her smiling face.

If you think you have a perfection rule, you can transform that rule into a guide this way:

1. State the rule precisely:
   - I *must* always do a perfect job.

2. Change *must* to *can*. Is it true?
   - I can *always* do a perfect job.

3. Change *always* to *sometimes*. Is it true?
   - I *can sometimes* do a perfect job.

4. Select three or more circumstances when you can follow the guide.
   - I can do a perfect job when:
     - I feel the job is important.
     - I have sufficient time.
     - The nature of the work permits it.

You can transform any rule into a guide. Perfection rules catch us all. Don't allow a perfection rule to prevent you from making progress on your job search.

11.3 Managing Impostor Syndrome

Sometimes, during a job search, you feel as if you're an impostor. Especially if it's been a while since you've had a job, you wonder if your past successes were real. Are you an impostor?

No, you are not an impostor.

You have had great experiences. If you feel you have not had enough experience, try an internship, an open-source project, or some other mechanism to obtain more experience.

Whatever you do, do *not* lie on your résumé. Do articulate your value for every position on your résumé. See the tips in Write Your Résumé, p. 67. Make sure you have references who can explain your value. And, ask for recommendations on LinkedIn. You might be pleasantly surprised by how other people see you.

11.4 I Can't Leave My Current Team

I talk to many team leaders and managers who—even though they are looking for a job—say a variant of, "I can't leave my current team right now; they depend on me."

Maybe you hired them. Maybe you're leading them. Maybe you're working for a startup. Whatever the case, you have an emotional contract, a *social* contract with these people, and you don't want to let them down.

Let me remind you of a hard fact. The company does not love you. Your team may hold you in high esteem. The people may follow you from organization to organization. They may even love you. But the company does not love you.

Here's the tough question:

Whose career is this?

You know the answer to that question: it's your career.

You can make choices about when to leave. You should provide two weeks of notice. That's the professional way to leave an organization.

Act professionally while you're fulfilling your remaining obligations to your current employer. Make sure you transition your work to other people. Make sure you leave that last day, knowing you found a place for all of your knowledge, as best you could.

Not Really In a Bind

A colleague asked for coaching. He'd started to look for a job. But he was concerned about leaving his team. Why?

"My team needs me."

I continued the five whys: "Why do they need you?"

"Because they aren't seasoned enough and the testing on the product will suffer."

"Why is that a problem?"

"Because the customers will report bugs. The company will suffer decreased sales."

"Why is that a problem?"

"The testers might get laid off."

"Why?"

"Because the company won't make enough money to keep paying them."

"So, you think by staying there, in a situation that you don't like, you can protect these other people's salaries? Is that it?"

"Yes."

I tried another tack, to see if I understood the problem clearly. "You said before the testers weren't seasoned enough, right?"

"Yes. I tried to bring in training several years ago."

"How many years ago?"

"Three years ago." He sighed. It was a very big sigh.

"And you never got the training?"

"No. That's why I'm looking for a new job. I got fed up."

I paused for a moment to let this sink in. He stared at me. His eyes welled up with tears.

"Staying isn't going to change anything, is it?" he asked me.

"I don't think so," I replied. "Will you be able to hire these testers if they get laid off?"

"Oh yes!"

My colleague was concerned about the effect his departure would have on his team. But he hadn't thought it through.

If you really have created a dependency on you, that's not a healthy situation, and you should leave, as quickly as possible. Everyone will be better off.

Yes, you will miss the people with whom you have created great friendships and great working relationships. And, if you find an even better situation, maybe you can hire them—eventually.

You have to be selfish about your career. No one else is going to be selfish about it. This is *your* career.

11.5 Keep Going; Don't Put Your Eggs All in One Basket

Until you have a written offer in your hand, keep going. The best place for a job hunter to be is to have offers coming in.

It's fine to say to an HR person or a hiring manager, "I'm expecting another offer this afternoon," or "I have to call back these other five people to tell them that I'm accepting your offer." When you're looking for a job, you never stop looking until you have a signed written offer.

You never stop looking even if you have a verbal offer. A verbal offer is not a real offer. A verbal offer is a promise. Promises can be broken. So it isn't a real offer until you get a written offer. On paper, that is signed. So you have to be careful not to stop looking until you get a signed, written offer.

11.6 I'll Just Apply Everywhere

 Don't use the "spray-and-pray" approach to sending your résumé. It doesn't work.

You are not perfect for every organization. Don't spray your résumé everywhere. Hiring managers can tell when you send a generic cover letter. They appreciate the candidate who makes the effort to send a letter highlighting why he or she is perfect for their open position. When you customize your cover letter, and make sure you send your résumé in the correct format, you pass the first hurdle.

You'll exhaust yourself if you apply everywhere. Use your judgment about where to apply. Use your non-application time to:

- Refine your résumé
- Update your target list of potential employers
- Update your target list of people you want to network with, so they can introduce you to people on your target list
- Update your LinkedIn profile (you do have a picture on your profile now, right?)
- Network with people online
- Network with people in person
- Write recommendations
- Ask for recommendations
- Ask for informational interviews
- Find a local networking group and start to attend meetings
- Know what your references are saying about you
- Get feedback and see if you are looking for a job that still exists
- You have plenty to do other than spray your résumé everywhere.

If you've been looking for a job for longer than three months, start with the checklist in It's Been Three Months. Now What?, p. 159.

11.7 If I Just Have the Perfect Résumé . . .

Another trap is thinking that if you just have the perfect résumé, people will find you.

You can spend a lot of time on your résumé. Spend *enough* time on your résumé. Ask people to look at your résumé and give you feedback on your résumé. But the perfect résumé probably does not exist.

Now you should spend time on your résumé articulating the value that you brought to the different jobs that you had. That's really the key. Where were you valuable in your different roles? As long as you explain your value you have a good résumé. And you should probably get help explaining that value.

But the perfect résumé is not going to get you the job. You still need a cover letter and an interview. Sometimes, you even need to articulate your value in an online application.

For every potential job, what's important to you as a candidate? What does the culture say to you? That's what you want to discuss in the cover letter and the interview. That's what you want to look for as you network for that referral. That's much more important than the résumé.

11.8 Should You Take Rejection Personally?

Every time you don't get a job it sure feels personal. And, in a way it is.

But, when you don't get the job, it's not a personal rejection, it's a candidate rejection. Remember, the company probably had 55 or 155 or 255 candidates for the position. And, even if you made it to the last two, it's not that they don't like you as a human being. It's that they liked the other candidate as a potential worker more.

To answer the question: try not to take the rejection personally.

This is a difficult time to maintain your self-esteem. It's very easy for me to say and much more difficult for you to do. So, you need to consider all the things you have to do for your physical and emotional health.

Think about how you attend to your physical and mental health while you are looking for a job. Especially if you no longer have that gym membership. You must prevent the downward emotional spiral. You must prevent looking desperate. Because, people do sense desperation and that does not make you an attractive candidate.

If you have trouble managing the rejection that is part of the job search, read The Recruiting Animal's *The Psychology of Job Hunting* (ANI13).

11.9 I Have Too Much Going On—Too Much Work In Progress

One of the problems I see each week is that some people have too much work in progress. Your data can help you here. Are you one of those people who has a ton of work in progress that never gets done? Are you starting a lot of things but you never get them finished? Is your Pen full of callbacks or email-backs?

If you have too much work in progress, you won't finish anything.

You have to limit the amount of work you have in progress so you can *make* progress. That's why you make your ToDos short. That's why you work in one-week timeboxes.

Make sure you keep retrospecting each week. You want to understand why you have started many tasks but not finished them. With your timeboxes and personal kanban, you will finish actions, not just start them. And, this is why you want the visibility of your personal kanban board, so you see all of your work in progress.

The reason to finish your tasks is to get feedback on them. Without feedback, you don't know if your experiment with this job fair or this résumé or this meeting or this Twitter search was worth the time you expended.

If you get feedback on your work you can say "Oh, I tried this. This thing was good, this one wasn't so good, this was okay. I looked at these kinds of companies, these were good for me, those were not good for me, but I have feedback on them." But, if you didn't finish your work, you won't get feedback and then you won't understand what organizations or managers or job fairs or interviews could be good for you. You won't have the feedback you need.

If you don't experiment, you don't get feedback. If you don't finish work, you don't finish the experiment. Are you finishing your experiments? Where are you getting feedback? Work in progress at the end of the week means you are not finishing things. It does not matter how much you start, it matters how much you finish. That's how you'll get the feedback.

When you plan for next week, put fewer tasks in the "Ready To Do" column. Only put in the number of tasks that you *accomplished* this week. Make sure all of the tasks are small, something you can accomplish in two hours or less. Check that you have the time in the upcoming week to complete all that work. If you don't, remove some of those tasks and put them on your Parking Lot. If you finish all of your ToDos, you can always pull in work from your backlog of tasks.

11.10 When You Don't Understand the Job Description

You would know if you were right for the job if hiring managers wrote a job analysis before they wrote a job description. But, since I am not the Empress of the Universe—at least, not yet—these poor hiring managers don't realize what a disservice they do to themselves and their candidates. It's easy to *not* understand job descriptions. Here are some hints:

- People use years of experience as a shorthand to mean "I don't want to train you."
- More years of experience often means more seniority.

- A laundry list of tools means you will need to use some tools and they don't know which ones—or HR doesn't know—so they threw in the kitchen sink.

The problem is that the hiring manager has not distinguished between the essential and non-essential technical and non-technical skills.

You have to decide what you will do. What value do you bring to employers?

If you have taken the time to Explain the Value of Every Item on Your Résumé, p. 69, you know the value you can deliver. If you Know Your Previous Job Patterns, p. 53, you know what has brought you satisfaction, and what hasn't. You have questions to ask for cultural fit.

Now, that might not get you in the door. But, being able to articulate your value to a potential employer, aside from being able to say you're a "high-energy" person? That's something quite useful. What if you said, "I'm not quite sure what this project management position is, but if you look at this position on my résumé, you can see I not only kept the sponsors engaged, but we delivered on time, saved the company an estimated $1 million per quarter in rework avoidance, and won a quality award"? You might garner some attention with that statement. Such as, "How did you do that?"

You still need to determine if it's worth your time to apply if you see a confusing job description.

11.11 I Can't Find a Job; I Should Go Back to School

I can sympathize with you. You've been looking for a while. You think you've been looking *everywhere*. And you just can't find a job. Maybe you should go back to school?

Look, if you want another degree, go for it. I have several degrees. But, I got my employers to pay for my Master's degree through tuition reimbursement. I didn't pay for it myself. Graduate school is expensive.

What if you need a course to show relevance in a certain area? Sure, pay for that yourself, if absolutely necessary to get a job. But an entire graduate program? My cynicism is showing.

This is a trap of insufficient networking. Or, it's a trap of looking for a job in a narrow way. It might be a LinkedIn profile that showcases you in a way that doesn't help the right hiring managers find you. Or, that your résumé is so narrow no one can imagine hiring you for anything else. Maybe you need some coaching or some other support.

Consider expanding your network. Rethink your résumé. Mind map your career. Those are three options I generated. What else could you do?

11.12 You Have a Zombie Profile on LinkedIn

Maybe you're between jobs or you're in school. Maybe you're just starting your job search. You're not sure what to put on your profile, so you don't have anything. You don't have a picture. You haven't filled any experience in. You don't even have your school details in your profile. You have an empty profile, a zombie profile.

If you have a zombie profile, especially a profile without a picture, you look scary to other people. Do not leave your zombie profile up and expect people to hire you or connect with you. You need to put some data into your profile.

Do this now. Before you do anything else. Otherwise, you are sabotaging your job search.

I wrote a blog post about this, called—what else—Don't Have a Zombie Profile on LinkedIn (ROT13).

11.13 You Have Imagined the Worst Thing That Could Happen

It happens to us all. We fall into low points during our job search, and we think, "Oh, I will *never* find a job." Or, you do the Five Whys, p. 41, and you decide all is lost. Or something terrifies you about your job search. Whatever it is, you have imagined the worst thing that could happen.

When this happens to you, it's time for risk management.

Back in Five Whys, I suggested these alternatives:

- Ask for an informational interview.
- Connect with someone on LinkedIn.
- Find three small ToDos. Make sure they are small. Put them on your "Ready To Do" column, so you have something for your next week.
- Use the Rule of Three for Generating More Ideas, p. 139.

In addition,

- Change your physical location. If you are in your home office, go outside. You don't have to go far.
- If you are listening to music, change what you are listening to. If you're listening to jazz, change it to classical or rock-and-roll.
- If you are making your ToDos electronically, change them to stickies.
- Go for a walk. Just ten minutes is good. Twenty minutes might be even better.
- Call a trusted colleague or a friend. Now is not a good time to be alone.

When you change your modality, you change how you perceive the world.

As for your next sticky, if you do not already have a networking group, create a sticky that says, "Find a local Networking Group." The one after that is, "Find out when and where they meet." The one after that is "Put the meeting on the calendar and go."

When you have imagined the worst, you need help from other people. You need a local networking group. You need to go to meetings.

Do some risk management. Once you have done that, you have managed the worst thing that could happen.

11.14 I Should Be Able to Do All of This Myself

I have left the biggest trap for last. A job search is never something anyone can do by themselves. You will need help from your family, friends, colleagues, and strangers. For some of us, asking for help is a huge emotional step. Let me reframe asking for help: It is a gift for the other person.

 Asking for help is a sign of emotional strength.

When you ask for help from other people, you offer them an opportunity to do something nice for you. The person offering help feels good. You gain the help, the other person feels good about him or herself. You have the opportunity to pay it forward sometime in the future.

When you offer help, you have a chance to help someone improve. And, when you learn how to take help, you can learn how to change your constraints. You might learn how to see success differently.

In a great economy, sure, maybe you don't need too much help to find a job. In a down economy? You need help.

What if you don't want to be associated with the person offering you help? Maybe you think the person is unethical? You can say, "Thank you." You don't have to call the people the unethical person sent you. It's that easy.

What if it's your mom or dad who wants to inflict help on you? That's a potential problem. If you really care, ask your parents:

- Are these people professionals in my field?
- Would these people look at me if I wasn't your child?
- Did you bribe these people to look at me?

If you believe your parents would answer honestly, ask the questions. Maybe you can treat these potential people as Loose Connections, p. 116 and see where the conversation takes you.

Ask for help, and do it from a place of emotional strength. Say to yourself, "This job search is a big complex project. I am taking advantage of all opportunities. I would be crazy to not ask for help from people who can help me. I will see what I can learn from these people." If you assume a learning stance, not a supplicant stance, you are more likely to succeed.

11.15 Now Do This

1. Which trap did you resonate most strongly with? What will you do about it?

2. How many times have you iterated on your résumé? Is that enough? What will be enough?

3. Look at your WIP. Are you trying to do too many things at once?

CHAPTER 12

Try These Tips

Does your job hunting need a little boost? These tips may help.

12.1 Make Your ToDos Small Enough to Complete in Two Hours or Less

Are you keeping your ToDos small? If you feel stuck, make your ToDos even smaller.

When you are searching for a job, you often find yourself with an hour or two between phone screens or interviews. You want to use that time. You have just enough time to research a company or a hiring manager. Or, just enough time to read a white paper. Or just enough time to prep for an interview. But you don't have enough time to complete something large, such as redrafting your résumé.

Redrafting your résumé is several ToDos: Write a first draft, get the résumé reviewed by a few trusted colleagues, edit it again, have more review, edit it yet again, have more review, maybe more edits. You might even decide to have multiple résumés, each one requiring more editing and review.

When you break "Redraft résumé" into "Write résumé draft 1" and "Get résumé draft 1 reviewed," you can be pretty sure both of those ToDos will be complete in a one-week timebox. Can you finish another round the same week? Maybe, maybe not. It depends on what else is on your ToDo list and how important it is. Is that first draft of your résumé good enough to send out? Maybe for some jobs. If it is good enough for most jobs, maybe you don't need to do another draft for a while. Maybe your time is more valuable spent elsewhere. Your sorted list of ToDos can help you determine this.

 If you suspect your tasks are too large, they are. Break them into smaller chunks. Moving tasks across the board will make you feel great. Your tasks are never too small. They can be too big.

If you are feeling stuck, make your ToDos smaller.

12.2 Learn How You Work and Manage Yourself

Back in Look for Quantitative Data, p. 33, I suggested that you might have to break apart tasks such as calling people if the call was a problem. You might be shy. You might be an introvert. You might hate the phone. You might have some other reason for not liking phone calls. But, you need to examine how you work best, and then manage yourself.

I'm an extrovert, and I don't like making phone calls. Why? Because they break up the day. However, you, as a job hunter, will *have* to make phone calls. So, become accustomed to making phone calls and having your day broken up.

I like working in time chunks of 30-60 minutes. I find that I am most productive in those time chunks. I can work in chunks of 10 minutes. And, when I have more time than that, I break the time into about one-hour chunks, just because I like it. So, I tend to group my calls together during the day. Then, when people call me back, sometimes, I get perturbed, because they interrupt me. I have to make sure I hit "save" and put on my smile when I answer the phone—because I initiated some outbound phone calls.

I have learned this about myself. You are a different person, and will discover what makes you most productive. I am sure you are different from me.

When you are in job-search mode, you might decide to devote an entire morning to phone calls. Or, an entire afternoon. I would. I would research and use LinkedIn and Twitter to connect with people because they are asynchronous forms of communication. And, when I want to connect, I would start in the morning. That way, I provide people an opportunity to reach me at my desk for the rest of the day.

To prepare for the phone calls, I might have to take notes on who I want to call, and what I want to say. Maybe I need cards next to the phone. Maybe I need a spreadsheet. Whatever I need to do, I want it all at my fingertips, so that when Rosemary or Margaret or Daniel or Cheng calls back I have the information. I can say, "Thank you for calling back, let me get my notes on your position—ah, here it is." A momentary pause is fine. Sounding like you are turning the house upside down is not.

This is why you need data.

12.3 Experiment with Different Companies

For a long time, I thought I was a small-company person. But a medium-size company was doing some very cool technology, and I wanted to be a part of it. So I found someone who would refer me, and I got a job there. (This is an example of selecting a target company.) I was happy there for five years, the longest I stayed anywhere as an employee. Guess I was wrong about being a small-company employee.

We all have biases about the kinds of companies or products or managers we think we might want or like when we start a job search. I encourage you to experiment in your job search with different kinds of companies. You don't know what kind of company is the best choice for you. In a great economy, you'll have many choices. In a down economy, you'll want to cast a very wide net.

You also want to make smart decisions about where you apply. Some organizations want you to fill out an online test before you fill out an online application, and you can't do 16 of those in a week, because it takes five hours to do each of those. So maybe, you want to timebox 30 minutes of research for each organization before you take the time to do a test and an application. Now, you're pretty sure you like the organization, you think it's worth your time to do the test and application, and you're sure you're right for the job. And, you're sure the organization will think so, too.

Not every organization has online tests and applications. Some ask you to send your résumé in a particular format. Do so. That's a form of a test. If you send your résumé in another format, you've flunked the test.

The key is to look at the job description and make sure it fits your qualifications. You want to finish your application and continue on to the next job. That way you have your candidacy in play in as many appropriate places as possible.

Before you apply, make sure you are right for the job. Don't waste your time on the trap, I'll Just Apply Everywhere, p. 126, also known as "spray-and-pray." Experimenting with different companies is different than applying everywhere.

Your criteria for a job are back in your values, which you defined in Mine Your Career Line.

12.4 Be Human and Remain Professional

You are a human being with a sense of humor. How do you let that sense of humor shine through and still be professional?

With a smile. And being careful on the phone. If you laugh, that's a hint that you have a sense of humor. Don't talk over the person on the other side of the phone call. But do let your sense of humor shine through. What are you going to do at work? Stifle your sense of humor, your sense of self? Go down into the basement once a day for your belly laugh? No, you are not. You must be *you* at work.

That said, you do want to be professional. You want your essence to shine through every interaction you have. Make sure you treat every interaction with every person as if he or she is a potential employer. Every single person. I am not saying to never let your guard down—far from it. I am saying you should be a gentleperson, period. With a sense of humor and a smile. Who wouldn't want to hire you?

Be your authentic self.

12.5 Use the Rule of Three for Generating More Ideas

Gerald Weinberg wrote about the Rule of Three in his classic text, *Secrets of Consulting* (WEI85):

> "If you can't think of three things that might go wrong with your plans, then there's something wrong with your thinking."

I like to turn the Rule of Three sideways and use it to generate more ideas, as in *Behind Closed Doors: Secrets of Great Management* (BCD05). With the Rule of Three, I assume there are at least three potential reasonable alternatives to the problem at hand. This helps generate ideas for networking, for what to do next, for problem solving with potential employers, for anything in your job search.

Here's the Rule of Three:

One idea is a trap.

Two ideas is a dilemma.

Three ideas starts to provide you options, and breaks logjam thinking.

You can often generate ideas four, five, six, and more, once you get past idea number three. But, if you're still stuck on idea #1 as your one and only idea, you are well and truly stuck. What are potential and reasonable ideas?

Turn the problem inside out and upside down. Brainstorm. Use your mindmap. That's three ideas for you. What else could you do?

12.6 Celebrate the Small Wins

You will land phone screens and interviews. Be happy about them. Celebrate them, even. That means that your perseverance is paying off. Then, get back to the work of your job search. Your job search isn't over until you have a written offer.

12.7 **Develop the Stories of Your Career**

Your career is composed of your stories—what you did at each job. I don't mean that you should make up stories. Not at all. I mean that you should know what you did. You should be able to take each accomplishment and be able to talk about it in a cohesive way.

Did you collaborate with a team and reduce the cost of a part? Or improve the process so that the organization saved millions of dollars? Or fixed a defect so the software released on time and improved customer satisfaction by some percentage and saved the company a gazillion dollars?

You want to be able to articulate the *value* of your work. That's what I mean by the stories of your career.

12.8 **Do Something Good Enough for Now**

Do not wait for anything to be perfect: your photo, your résumé, your twitter page, *anything*. When you start job hunting, the important thing is to start. This is an example of the growth mindset (DWE07).

If you do something good enough for now, you have accomplished *something*. You can iterate on that thing later. You can turn your attention to the next highest priority on your ToDo list, instead of polishing that good-enough thing that you already accomplished.

Here's an example. Say you decided to write a draft of your résumé. Maybe you decided to spend three hours on it. You're done, and you sent it to three trusted colleagues for review. You're done for now.

Now you can turn your attention to the next ToDo. Maybe that ToDo is "List the in-person networking places for this month." That's a critical ToDo. How else will you meet people? If you don't list them, you can't even make a decision. Your résumé is good enough for now. It's in review. You are done with *that* for now. Sure, your colleagues will find problems. You hope they will, right?

You have put your résumé aside for now, in favor of other work to accomplish on your job search. As you should.

That's the point of doing something good enough for now. You'll get better at your résumé over time, because you have the growth mindset.

12.9 How to Use a Recruiter in Your Job Search

If you're looking for a job, and you have more than two years of experience, you can consider using a recruiter. Some recruiters have entry-level jobs, but that's rare in this economy.

The more experience you have, the more senior you are, and the more specialized your experience is, the more you need a recruiter. You are more likely to be looking for a position that is unique and less likely to be advertised.

So how do you find and use a recruiter?

12.9.1 *Use Someone Who Helped You Find a Position Before*

Did you find your current or most recent position through a recruiter? Was it a good experience? Call that person again. If your experience was not good, don't call that person.

Ask your friends for their references. Ask your LinkedIn colleagues for their references. Ask people who have found positions through recruiters who they like. Word-of-mouth referrals for recruiters are the best kind of referral.

You can even ask the hiring managers in your organization which recruiters they use, although that starts to put the recruiter in a sticky situation if you are still employed.

12.9.2 *Use Someone Sourcing for Your Open Positions Now*

If you've been a hiring manager, an easy choice is to use a recruiter you've trusted to find the right people for your department. But, you must be careful if you are in the middle of hiring others for your department and looking for a new job yourself. You don't want to put the recruiter in a no-win position. Discuss this with the recruiter.

Ask the recruiter if he or she has jobs at the level you want. Not all recruiters have jobs at all levels. Maybe you are not qualified for the level you want. You need to work with someone who will provide you with honest feedback. You may need someone in the same organization as your current recruiter, but not someone who is sourcing for your open positions.

12.9.3 *What About a Recruiter Who Cold-Calls You?*

Some of my best ongoing relationships through the years have been with recruiters who cold-called me. They had heard of me, as a senior engineer, or as a manager who had open reqs, so they called. I listened to some of them. When I was a hiring manager, I let them prove themselves to me. I now have a short list of trusted Boston-area recruiters, who I recommend and/or provide referrals for.

12.9.4 *Good Recruiters are Not Like Bad Car Salespeople*

Yes, recruiters are salespeople. Yes, they serve the hiring organization. And, that doesn't mean that you can't both win from a long and lasting relationship. Bad salespeople exist in all industries. And, the great recruiters are not like the bad car salespeople, or like ambulance-chasing lawyers. You can trust great recruiters.

I cultivate my recruiting colleague relationships. I refer people to them. In exchange, I hear about new positions early, increasing my value to my network. I can't always make a connection. When I do, it's great.

If you are senior enough, consider a recruiter. Choose one recruiter, maybe two. Do not use more than two recruiters at a time—they will be showing you the same jobs, especially in a down economy. Decide how long you want to give the recruiting relationship. If at the end of that time you're not happy, end the recruiting relationship and move to another recruiter. And, consider the feedback the recruiter has provided. Are you taking advice on your dress, your résumé, your interview style? Because, your inability to land a job could be about *you*, not the recruiter.

Recruiters can help you iterate on everything in your search, if you let them. They can hold up a mirror, if you let them. The question is this: Will you?

12.10 Do Something Every Day

I bet that some days you wake up and say, "Oh, I just can't take it. I cannot do anything on my job search today." If you're still working full time, this is especially a big problem. And, if you've been looking for a long time and not finding anything, you might feel quite dejected.

Take ten minutes and do *something*.

It doesn't matter what it is. Make sure you have small ToDos. Make sure you can move one ToDo across the board.

Why? You will feel as if you've accomplished something. You will feel more energized. That one movement will help you tackle your job search the next day.

Do something today.

12.11 Now Do This

1. Are you on LinkedIn yet? If not, get on LinkedIn now. I'll wait.
2. Develop some of the stories of your career so you can answer some interview questions.
3. Are you managing your work so that you can accomplish both the phone calls and the desk work?
4. Do something today.

PART V

Special Circumstances: New Grad, Career Transition, Over 50

CHAPTER 13
What You Need to Know if You Are in Transition

You are in transition if you are a new grad or you are making a transition to a new career.

In some ways, being a new grad is easy. You don't have any "bad" experience to overcome—except maybe that internship. That's because some managers don't consider internships "real" experience. Whatever the case, internships provide you with leads for your network and some real-world experience. If you had an internship, mine those connections first for your job search.

If you are in a career transition, you have some of the same problems as a new grad. However, you can offer a hiring manager maturity—which the manager might see as a good thing. In either case, you share some of the same problems that a new grad has. Here are some tips that might help.

13.1 Get Your Foot in the Door

You need to get your foot in the door, and work for those first two critical years, to get that initial real-employee experience. Because, until you have a minimum of two years of experience on your résumé, you are still an entry-level employee. And, that's a difficult place to be.

13.2 Networking for People New to a Field

For the first two years of your career, pay special attention to building your network. You have the opportunity to network with people every day at work. You've probably been meeting people everywhere at work. Build your network every day.

As you meet people, add them to your LinkedIn list as you feel is appropriate. One of the things that I suggest to people who are young in their career is to make sure that you attend professional or user group meetings to start building your network.

13.3 Network at Professional Meetings

What local professional meetings can you attend?

You might think of attending these meetings for recertification units, although I think of recertification as a nice side benefit. You want to attend these meetings to build a warm connection with people and to build your network.

Don't go because the first person you meet might give you the best possible job. Go because you might learn something—and to network.

You cannot tell who you are going to meet at these meetings, but you might meet some very interesting people. You're probably going to learn something very interesting, and not always from the speaker.

 Professional meetings are great networking opportunities.

You will learn something from the person sitting next to you. You will learn that you're not alone in the concerns and risks that you have in your job. You will learn that people are solving similar problems in very interesting ways. You will learn that there are conferences coming up that you can attend. And you should come away from those meetings with business cards.

Not because you need to collect business cards and throw them in your desk, but because you want to add these people to your LinkedIn list. Networking with people and adding people to your LinkedIn list is something you need to do all the time, even if you are currently employed. This sounds like a really strange idea that you want to be a collector of people, but you do!

Don't throw the business cards in your desk. Invite those people to connect with you on LinkedIn with a personal message.

These are the people who become your loose connections, with whom you can network and find your next job.

That is why you need to meet them, that is why you need to see them, so that you go to the next meeting, the C user group meeting, or the Java user group meeting, and you say "Hey, Steve, it's nice to see you again. How's life? The last time we spoke you were having trouble with the server, you were having trouble with whatever, the configuration management system. How was that resolved?" And Steve will say, "Oh that is so nice of you to remember that." You have a little conversation. Even if you don't see Steve for another few months, he remembers you the next time and you have another little conversation.

 Attend enough meetings to create relationships.

You're professional colleagues. You remember each other. You don't have to have too many acquaintances like that to build your professional network. Then in a few years when you have to look for another job you say, "Steve, remember me?" Yes, he remembers you. And with warmth and fondness, not like you were a good friend, but with enough warmth that he says, "Oh I remember you and you know what? There's a job that might be perfect for you over here." That's the kind of networking you want.

That's why you need to be going to these meetings. You don't need to go to a meeting every single night of the week. You need to go to enough of them often enough so that you can network with people. This works well when you have enough experience so that you know what groups you can go to. Choose the meetings that make sense for you.

Go to meetings in your field. If you're smart, you go to a few meetings that might not be in your field. There are plenty of meetings.

Look for mashups, meetups, anything like that in your local area. Do not stay home every single night of the week. Look for a meeting at least once or twice a month and start going. This is how you build your network.

13.4 Sit With People You Don't Know

Do not sit with all of your friends. Find a table; find a place to sit next to at least one person you don't know. Say "Hello," and smile. Extend your hand, no limp-fish handshakes! Firm handshakes. And smile and say, "Hi, my name is . . . (insert your name here)." And then just let the conversation flow.

I have numeric goals when I go to meetings. I want to meet two or three people tonight that I have not met before. Maybe you don't need a goal.

If you don't know how to meet people, go to one of the organizers and say, "I would like your help. I would like to meet one or two people here tonight." And they will say, "Okay, I will help!"

If nothing else, you can go to the speaker and say, "It's so nice to meet you. My name is (whatever your name is)." And you can meet the speaker. The speaker is there because the speaker wants to *meet* people. That's what speakers do. So, there is always an opportunity to meet people that you don't know. Use that.

This is when you have a couple years of experience, you know your topic; you know your domain. So you've been networking all along. You're collecting people and you have a nice network.

If you are a hiring manager and you've been doing this all along, this is a way for people to get to know you. And, if you are suddenly on the other side looking for a job, now you can exploit your network because you have been looking for people all along. Now it should be very easy for you to go and tell people, "Hey I'm now looking for a job. Do you know of anybody looking for someone like me?"

You have been nice to people all along, you've been courteous, you've been polite, and you've been helping them find jobs. These people should be bending over backwards to help you look for a job. All of your helpfulness should pay off.

13.5 **Work for Free, for Now**

You do not have to work for free as a full-time job. In fact, you *should* not. Do not let anyone take advantage of you. If you work, you should be paid for your work.

However, when you transition from school to work, consider working for free *for a short time* in the form of internships, volunteer work, open-source volunteering—building your skill set doing philanthropic projects. You can grow contacts and build your work portfolio all at the same time. The people with whom you work should be willing to connect with you on LinkedIn and provide you with references. If they are not, ask why not.

Some people I know have volunteered at their church or synagogue and have parlayed that work into full-time work based on referrals and recommendations. When you show your expertise in one setting, it can pay off. Be careful about how much time you invest in a non-paying "opportunity." Other people call them opportunities. I call them opportunities to take advantage of you.

13.6 **Add More Loose Connections**

Did you have jobs in high school or college? If so, make sure you add those people to your LinkedIn network. See if you can get those people to write you recommendations on LinkedIn.

Did you have a great relationship with a college advisor? Connect with that person on LinkedIn and ask for a recommendation.

Do connect with your friends. Don't ask them for recommendations.

Do network with your friends. At the very beginning of your careers, you might not be very helpful to one another, but a few years in, you might be very helpful. In fact, if you're feeling shy, bring a friend to a professional meeting. That's even better than going alone. So buddy up—if you can—to participate in professional society meetings.

13.7 Live Where You Have Options, if You Can

If you are just out of school and you have a BA in something that does not *directly* lead to a job, make sure you live in or near a large city. Why? Because you need to have many options.

If you are not from a large city, find a couch to crash on, take an hourly job in a large city, and make enough money waitressing or bussing tables or doing something that will allow you to search for a professional job in your off hours. If you are lucky, and you thought about your search far enough ahead, you could have started your search while you were in school. If not, start now. And, stop worrying. You have a system and a plan. Settle down and get to work.

13.8 Now Do This

1. How do you want to network to build your connections? Are there meetings, mashups, other in-person events that make sense for you?
2. How will you ask for recommendations?
3. How will you build loose connections?

CHAPTER 14
Just for People Over 50

I wish I could tell you age discrimination was a figment of your imagination. It's not. It's real. But you can manage some of the issues in age discrimination, if you are smart about your job search.

14.1 Networking for People Over 50

If you're over the age of 50, you still want to be able to build your network. Even if you ignored your network until now, it's just a little harder. This is really important if you have been, shall we say, a little geeky.

One of the things that some of us have done, over the course of our professional lives, especially if we've been technical professionals, is think we didn't have to look for our jobs. Our jobs would come to us. And the more technical we've been, the less we always had to look for jobs. In a down economy? Hah! All bets are off.

So, *especially* if you're over 50, and you've been technical all of your life, and now you're suddenly looking for a job, and you realize you only have 30 contacts on LinkedIn: this is a real shock to your system. So, add everyone you know on LinkedIn as a contact. Yes, everyone you know from your religious affiliation, everyone you know in your family, everyone you know that you ever worked with. This could take a while. You might want to break this up into several ToDos, with the most recent job first, so you can decide which of your other job search tasks are more important, as you continue to build your network.

Go down the list of everyone you ever worked with in all of your jobs. Make sure you fill out your profile on LinkedIn and make sure that you add people to your LinkedIn contact list. You have probably worked with hundreds of people. This is good. Find them. Add them.

Reread the Network, Network, Network chapter, p. 101. Add yourself to the alumni email lists and LinkedIn groups of the companies you have worked for, whether you were a contractor or an employee. If you have gone to different schools, add yourself to the alumni email lists and groups for the schools. You need to do this, because this is how you will network for your next job.

14.2 Decide How You Will Manage Ageism

You will have to decide how you will deal with ageism. Some people will tell you to dye your hair. I'm not going to tell you to do that. Some people will tell you not to say when you graduated from college. People who read your résumé can add so I'm not going to tell you to omit dates.

I *will* tell you to be ready to take jobs as a contractor rather than as an employee. Some people think that "Oh, you're 55. You only have 10 more years to work." Well, I don't know what they think is going to happen in those 10 years; you're going to drop dead? I don't think so.

Those of us in our 50s will still be working until we are 70 or 75. So, feel free to take jobs as a contractor or permanent employee. And, offer that option to potential employers. Don't feel as though you have to take a permanent job, and feel free to increase your potential wage rate so that you can pay for your own healthcare and other benefits. But if it makes your potential employers feel better because you're offering to take a job as a contractor instead of an employee, do that.

Remember, all you need to do is land that interview, so offer to take the job as a contractor in your cover letter, especially if you have the relevant experience. Make sure you charge enough to offset the loss in benefits.

14.3 **Problem-Solve with a Potential Employer**

You may have to be ready to provide options to a potential employer. Consider suggesting options to your interviewing managers. "Well, maybe you don't want me to be a technical lead, but what about a project coordinator?"

When I went back to work after my second child, I took a job as a technical test automation developer. I had been a Director of Development, and I chose to write automated tests. I was under 50 at the time, but I chose to do more technical work because I wanted to increase my developer skills, and I wanted to make sure I understood the technical skills involved when I decided to return to management. Maybe you can consider a highly technical position also?

No matter what, use the Rule of Three for Generating More Ideas, p. 139. You can use the Rule of Three for yourself and with a potential employer, if you have discovered a cultural fit, but not a firm job fit.

14.4 **Demonstrate Relevance**

The older you are, the more important it is for you to show that you are *relevant*. Demonstrate your relevance with current methodologies and technologies. If you were not able to stay current in your most recent position, volunteer for a local association, or perform some open source work. Then, add that to your résumé and to your LinkedIn profile.

14.5 **Look for a Technical or Line Position**

The more technical or directly involved with the business of the organization you are, the more useful you are to a potential employer.

That's what I mean by a "line" position. I don't mean an assembly line job; I mean a "not-staff" job. Staff jobs that serve supportive roles such as human resources or finance or even IT in an engineering organization don't *directly* contribute to the company's revenue. The company considers them "staff" jobs. You can tell if a job is a staff job if it has its own cost center, or worse, comes under the heading of "General Administration and Overhead."

In a software organization, technical experience—developer, tester, even project manager—is more valuable than managerial experience. There are more developer and tester jobs than there are manager jobs. Can you still write code? Look for a developer job rather than a manager job.

Don't look for a staff job, such as process improvement specialist, or assistant to something. If you have been in management for a long time and you don't have technical skills anymore, and you don't want a technical position, then keep looking for a management job. But the older you are, the more important it is to show your technical skills. You might need to take a course to prove you still have technical chops, but that's a small price to pay for actually getting a job, right?

If you have had staff positions your entire career, this may be a shock to your system. For example, if you have been in IT, I'm suggesting you consider Engineering or R & D. Or, look for a job where IT *is* the business of the organization. Big change. Can you make this change? Maybe it's time for you to consider an open-source project to try an experiment and gain some feedback.

14.6 Now Do This

1. Be creative about potential jobs. Consider brainstorming alternatives with a hiring manager.
2. Consider contract work.
3. Develop at least three potential jobs you can hunt for. How would a company describe those jobs? Look for them.

PART VI
What to Do When Your Job Search Takes Longer than Three Months

Even when you have a system in place to manage your job search, sometimes it takes longer than three months to find a job. Try these ideas.

CHAPTER 15
It's Been Three Months. Now What?

You've been diligently using timeboxes and personal kanban. You've been building your LinkedIn network. You've been networking in person. You've asked for feedback. You've had some interviews. But you *still* don't have a job. It's been three months or more. Now what?

15.1 Verify Your Basics With This Checklist

First, make sure that you can check everything off this checklist:

1. You have a picture on your LinkedIn profile. Remember, people who have a picture are seven times more likely to get picked by hiring managers than people who don't.
2. Your LinkedIn profile summary line says you are looking for a job.
3. LinkedIn thinks your profile is complete.
4. You have at least three recommendations on LinkedIn.
5. You have joined all of your alumni groups on LinkedIn: university and corporate.
6. You have a target list of potential employers and you are working on meeting people from that list.
7. You have increased your connections weekly.
8. You are asking for informational interviews, at least a couple every week.
9. You have joined a networking group, such as WIND.
10. You are looking for jobs on Twitter.
11. You are using stickies or cards for your personal kanban.

12. You are using a one-week timebox.
13. You are gathering data each week about your ToDos.
14. Your ToDos are small. You can complete each of them inside of two hours, more of them in less than two hours.
15. Your ToDos are independent.
16. You are monitoring your WIP.
17. You are reflecting each week about your previous week.

The reason I want you to continue to use stickies or cards is that the tactile feel of the stickies or cards helps you choose what to do. When teams use stickies or cards, they create a shared mental model of the story. You are not part of a team. You alone need to decide what to do and when to do it. And, if you have a job, you have less time to devote to your job search than people looking full time. You need to use your time wisely. The stickies or cards will help you decide.

A one-week timebox is enough time to accomplish work but not so much time that you have time to postpone work. It allows you to gather data about your work so you can get feedback that you can use for the next week.

If you have not accomplished everything on the checklist, why not? What is holding you back? You have an impediment. Here's what one colleague said to me about the lack of his picture on his LinkedIn profile:

> "I can't use a picture on my LinkedIn profile. I'm in the *security* business. No one will take me seriously." My friend was concerned.

> "That's not an answer. Here's a potential hiring manager. That guy has a picture," I retorted.

> "Well, that guy doesn't know about security."

> "That guy has a job," I answered.

You have to balance what is reasonable in your business with what is reasonable for a hiring manager. Even hiring managers who are in the security business.

15.2 **What Does the Data Tell You?**

If you reflect each week, you will have data about your previous week. If you are not excited about where you have applied, or your results, you have options. You can change your résumé. You can change your LinkedIn profile. You can reconsider your answers to interview questions.

Do NOT lie when you answer questions. By now, three or more months into your job search, you've had a chance to practice interviewing. You and I know that too many interviewers ask questions that are not behavior-description questions. You can practice your interviewing without having an interview. This is where a networking support group might be helpful.

Here are some questions for you:

1. Are you looking for a job that will help you succeed? Look back at your career timeline and your answers when you mined the data. Do the jobs you're looking for help you move forward? Or are they sideways jobs? Or worse, backwards jobs?
2. Are there any jobs in your desired field? Or, are you like the travel agents of the 1980s? Are you looking for a job that no longer exists?
3. Are people only looking at you based on past experience that you want to move away from? Do you feel as if you've been typecast?

Let's take each of these. You might have a different problem. But maybe these problems and their solutions can unwedge your thinking.

15.3 **Your Interviews Seem to be for Lateral Positions**

You thought you were humming along in your career. And then you were laid off, so now you're looking for a job. And, this job search is taking longer than you thought. The jobs you're finding aren't an improvement. They're a lateral move. Even worse, some of them seem to be a step down. What's going on?

Well, maybe you weren't progressing as fast as you thought. Or, if there was a significant layoff in your town, there are too many qualified people for the same few jobs. Your career is going to suffer. Too much supply, not enough demand. I could tell you not to take it personally, but it's your life. Go ahead and take it personally. I would.

If you are committed to that geographical location, and it's not a big city, such as New York or Boston or Chicago—yes, I mean a really big city, then you might have to consider a different position or a smaller job or less money. Alternatively, you can move to a different geographical location where the local labor market is not so inundated with talented people.

If you are in a big labor market, and you're still looking at lateral jobs, you need feedback from a recent interview. Ask one or more of the interviewers for feedback from a job you didn't land. You have nothing to lose. I would send an email asking for an informational interview, saying something like this, after the Dear So-and-so,

> I enjoyed our interview. I was disappointed to not get the job. I would like some feedback from you because I have not landed any job in the past five months, and I'm wondering why. Do you have 15 minutes to debrief with me? I could use your expertise. Thanks very much.

Have a list of questions ready. You might start with these questions:

- What did you expect of me that I did not deliver?
- What technical skills did I not exhibit?
- What leadership skills were you looking for that I didn't show you?
- What other skills did I not show?

Do not argue. Do not forget to thank the interviewer for his or her time. You are gathering data.

If you believe you have the skills required for the job, you need to sharpen your interviewing skills. Yes, it is possible that the people who interview you are terrible interviewers. Tough. You need to show them how good you are despite their lack of skill.

15.4 You are Looking for a Low-Volume Job or a Non-Existent Job

Maybe you are looking for a job that still exists, but there are so few people hired for it every year, it's practically *nonexistent*. I'm thinking about Fortran and Cobol programmers. Cobol and Fortran programmers can make a living—but the jobs are limited.

However, in my mind, a programmer is a programmer. If you insist on putting a particular language in front of it, that's when you encounter problems.

You might need to be more adaptable than you originally thought. If you were a developer, can you imagine a job as a test developer, developing test automation?

If you were an auditor, can you imagine a job as a tester, trading in a staff position for a line position?

If you were a business analyst, can you imagine working with a product owner? If you were a product manager, can you imagine becoming a business analyst?

The jobs are not the same. No, sirree. But they are not so far off. And, depending upon the size of the organization, they might be quite related to what you did before. Remember, no one's career is linear.

Do not become stuck in thinking you need to have the same job you had before. That job is gone. It might never return. You need a new job.

15.5 You are Being Typecast

If you can only get interviews for a narrow set of jobs, you need to look at your network, your LinkedIn profile, and your résumé.

The tighter your network, i.e., the more your network revolves around the same area, the more your network will reinforce itself and the more difficult it will be to break out and find other positions. People will say, "Oh, I know Kris. He's great at whatever you're great at." They will never look at you for anything else. You will have to take significant actions for them to realize that you can do other things.

Those actions could be starting a blog, public speaking, or writing articles to show your expertise. But that's time-intensive. It might be easier to expand your network. Which you need to do to find a job.

Review your LinkedIn profile and your résumé. How do you showcase your talents so that the type of work you want to do is highlighted? You can be proud of your accomplishments. And you need to show you have the necessary skills, experience, and knowledge to do a particular job.

15.6 Persevere

No matter what, keep going. Use the feedback you gain from your interviews, your reflections, your networking, everything about your job search to be successful. And, don't be afraid to ask for help. Very few people find their next job alone.

Remember the power of loose connections. Networking, showing your value on your résumé, and continuing to learn from your experiences will help.

Use the structure of timeboxes and personal kanban to make your job search work for you. I wish you the best.

15.7 Now Do This

1. Review the checklist. Make sure you are sticking with the kanban and see if your results change.
2. Gather data on your networking. How many people did you add to your network last week? Start tracking your data.
3. Try to diagnose your problem and see if it's any of the problems I've outlined here. If so, start here. If not, ask for help from a colleague.

Glossary

If you are not familiar with the terms I've used, here are the definitions:

Agile: You work in small chunks, finishing work that is valuable to the customer in the order the customer specifies. The value of working in an agile way is that you have the ability to change quickly, because you complete work.

Kanban: Literally the Japanese word for "signboard." A scheduling system for limiting the amount of work in progress at any one time.

Lean: A pull approach to managing work that looks for waste in the system.

LinkedIn: A social networking website for people in professional occupations. http://www.linkedin.com.

Parking Lot: This is a place to put issues you don't want to lose but don't necessarily want to address at this time.

Pen: In personal kanban, the place to corral ToDos that can get lost.

Timebox: A specific limited amount of time in which the person will attempt to accomplish a specific task.

WIP or Work in Progress: Any work that is not complete. When you think in lean terms, it is waste in the system.

Annotated Bibliography

[AMA11] Amabile, Teresa and Steven Kramer. *The Progress Principle: Using Small Wins to Ignite Joy, Engagement, and Creativity at Work*. Boston: Harvard Business Review Press, 2011. Just in case you don't believe me, there's research that says we like to finish work in small chunks so we can make progress.

[ANI13] Animal, Recruiting. *The Psychology of Job Hunting: Transform yourself from a lily-livered loser into a Sales Man*. Canada: Recruiting Animal, 2013. An ebook that helps you navigate the issues of selling yourself in the the job hunting world. Recruiting Animal is a Canadian recruiter with an internet talk show. I think he's a riot. You might not. But his book? On target.

[BEN11] Benson, Jim and Tonianne DeMaria Barry. *Personal Kanban Mapping Work | Navigating Life*. CreateSpace, 2011. This is the book that really explains how to use personal kanban in an easy-to-understand way. I read the book, internalized it, and did not realize that I was quoting from it. That's how easy it is to understand, internalize, and adopt personal kanban. You can drop the personal from that sentence, too, and apply the principles as kanban in projects at work.

[BUC99] Buckingham, Marcus, and Curt Coffman. *First, Break All the Rules: What the World's Greatest Managers Do Differently*. New York: Simon & Schuster, 1999. An eye-opening look to what great managers do.

[DER06] Derby, Esther and Diana Larsen. *Agile Retrospectives: Making Good Teams Great.* Dallas and Raleigh: Pragmatic Bookshelf, 2006. If you need ideas for any retrospective or reflection, this is the book to use. No, they don't pay me for this endorsement. But they should!

[DWE07] Dweck, Carol. *Mindset: The New Psychology of Success.* New York: Ballantine Books, 2007. This book discusses the fixed mindset and the growth mindset. If you have the fixed mindset, you believe you can only do what you were born with. If you have the growth mindset, you believe you can acquire new skills and learn. I believe in the growth mindset. So should you. It's how you get better, bit by bit. Sound familiar?

[HEA13] Heath, Chip and Dan Heath. *Decisive: How to Make Better Choices in Life and Work.* New York: Crown Business Books, 2013. If you need more discussion than just "The Rule of Three," use this book to help you understand how to make better choices. I have used this approach in my coaching and consulting with my clients.

[LEI13] Leipzig, Adam. *How to Know Your Life Purpose in 5 Minutes.* https://www.youtube.com/watch?v=vVsXO9brK7M. 2013. I was surprised at how quickly these five questions get to the point. Because they are not about *you*, but about the *people* you serve, they work.

[LES09] Lester, Andy. *Land the Tech Job You Love.* Dallas and Raleigh: Pragmatic Bookshelf, 2009. Andy delves into the necessary detail about how to write your résumé, how to write a cover letter, and how to interview. I've scratched the surface and described a framework. Andy has the depth behind the framework.

[OHN88] Ohno, Taiichi. *Toyota Production System: Beyond Large-Scale Production.* New York: Productivity Press, 1988. Taiichi Ohno discusses the notions of teamwork, just-in-time, and especially the ideas of *pulling* work, rather than *pushing* work through the system. I originally read this book when I was reading about how to apply these ideas to unwedging my clients in software and software/hardware organizations. Then, the lightbulb went on. I could use it for me.

[PFE10] Pfeffer, Jeffrey. *Power: Why Some People Have It and Others Don't.* New York: HarperCollins, 2010. I don't agree with everything Pfeffer says, but he always makes me think. I do agree with what he says about networking. Like I said, he makes me think. He'll make you think, too.

[PIE06] Pierson, Orville. *The Unwritten Rules of the Highly Effective Job Search.* New York: McGraw-Hill Inc., 2006. A terrific marketing plan for the job seeker. Although the author calls this a project plan, it's a marketing plan of how to determine your target list, your core message, and how to react when you realize you are looking for a job that is scarce. I wish it had references.

[PIN09] Pink, Dan. *Drive: The Surprising Truth About What Motivates Us.* New York: Riverhead Books, 2009. This is a link to Dan Pink's TEDTalk about what motivates us: purpose, mastery, and autonomy. He explains why financial incentives alone don't work. Yes, you need to make enough money, but money isn't enough to keep you satisfied. This is why you can't just use money as a decision for your job search. Well, you can, but you may well not be satisfied.

[RAT07] Rath, Tom. *StrengthsFinder 2.0.* Washington D.C. and Omaha: Gallup Press, 2007. The book is a list of strengths, what I would call attributes, or qualities, preferences, and skills. The value is in the code you get when you buy the book. You use the code to take a StrengthsFinder assessment, which allows you to develop and discover your natural talents.

[ROT12] Rothman, Johanna. *Hiring Geeks That Fit.* Practical Ink, 2012. If you want to know how to hire people, this is it, from soup to nuts. All the templates are available for free on my website. The book explains how to use them.

[BCD05] Rothman, Johanna and Esther Derby. *Behind Closed Doors: Secrets of Great Management.* Dallas and Raleigh: Pragmatic Bookshelf, 2005. We describe the Rule of Three and many other management approaches and techniques in here.

[ROTH07] Rothman, Johanna. *Manage It! Your Guide to Modern, Pragmatic Project Management.* Dallas and Raleigh: Pragmatic Bookshelf, 2007. If you want to know more about how to estimate task size, establish a project rhythm, or see a project dashboard, this is the book for you. I have references about why multitasking is crazy in here.

[ROT09] Rothman, Johanna. *Manage Your Project Portfolio: Increase Your Capacity and Finish More Projects.* Dallas and Raleigh: Pragmatic Bookshelf, 2009. In many ways, you are managing a project portfolio, except that you are managing a project portfolio of just job-finding work. This book helps you manage all the work in your project portfolio. I also have more references about why multitasking is crazy in here.

[ROT13] Rothman, Johanna. *Don't Have a Zombie Profile on LinkedIn,* http://www.jrothman.com/blog/htp/2013/07/dont-have-a-zombie-profile-on-linkedin.html. Why you need to have a bare-bones LinkedIn profile.

[SAL11] Saltpeter, Miriam, *How to be Found on LinkedIn,* http://money.usnews.com/money/blogs/outside-voices-careers/2011/12/15/how-to-be-found-in-linkedin. Read it, and see if you area doing what the experts say you should be doing.

[STA00] Stanfield, R. Brian, Editor. *The Art of Focused Conversation, 100 Ways to Access Group Wisdom in the Workplace.* Canada: New Society Publishers, 2000. This is the book that explains how to have a focused conversation.

[WEI13] Weinberg, Gerald M. "Seeing Your Own Big Picture," in Esther Derby *et al.*, in *Readings for Problem-Solving Leadership.* Leanpub, 2013. How to go meta.

[WEI85] Weinberg, Gerald M. *The Secrets of Consulting*. New York: Dorset House Publishing, 1985. If you're thinking of becoming a consultant, you should read this classic text. Full of rules and aphorisms, you will learn what to do as a consultant. You will also learn, just by reading, if you do *not* want to be a consultant. Cheap learning.

[WEI86] Weinberg, Gerald M. *Becoming a Technical Leader: An Organic Problem-Solving Approach*. New York: Dorset House, 1986. If you only read one book a year about how to become the best leader you can be, this is the book to read. I teach Problem Solving Leadership every year with Jerry and Esther Derby, and we often refer to this book when we teach. I learn every time I teach. You will learn every time you read.

[WHI10] Whitcomb, Susan Britton; Bryan, Chandlee; and Deb Dib. *The Twitter Job Search Guide: Find a Job and Advance Your Career in Just 15 Minutes a Day*. Indianapolis: Jist Works, 2010. I was tempted to write 140 characters about this book. I decided you deserved a little more. The book is already dated, not surprisingly. If you decide to use Twitter as a primary search mechanism for your job search, do get this book. On the other hand, I would build my target list first, because that's a better use of my job search time.

More from Johanna

I consult, speak, and train about all aspects of managing product development. I have a distinctly *agile* bent. I'm more interested in helping you become more effective than I am in sticking with some specific approach. There's a reason my newsletter is called the "Pragmatic Manager"—that's because I am!

If you liked this book, you might also like the other books I've written:

Agile and Lean Program Management: Collaborating Across the Organization[1]
Hiring Geeks That Fit[2]
Manage Your Project Portfolio: Increase Your Capacity and Finish More Projects[3]
Manage It!: Your Guide to Modern, Pragmatic Project Management[4]
Behind Closed Doors: Secrets of Great Management[5]

In addition, I have essays in:

Readings for Problem-Solving Leadership[6]
Center Enter Turn Sustain: Essays on Change Artistry[7]

---

[1]https://leanpub.com/agileprogrammanagement
[2]https://leanpub.com/hiringgeeks
[3]http://pragprog.com/book/jrport/manage-your-project-portfolio
[4]http://pragprog.com/book/jrpm/manage-it
[5]http://pragprog.com/book/rdbcd/behind-closed-doors
[6]https://leanpub.com/pslreader
[7]https://leanpub.com/changeartistry

I'd like to stay in touch with you. If you don't already subscribe, please sign up for my email newsletter, the Pragmatic Manager[8], on my website. Please do invite me to connect with you on LinkedIn[9], or follow me on Twitter, [@johannarothman].

I would love to know what you think of this book. If you write a review of it somewhere, please let me know. Thanks!

—Johanna

---

[8]http://www.jrothman.com/pragmaticmanager/
[9]http://www.linkedin.com/in/johannarothman

Index

A

about.me pages, 68

accomplishments, including in
  résumés, 69–70

actions. *See* ToDos

adaptability, 163–164

age discrimination, 153, 154

agile and lean principles, 31

alumni networks, 101–105

applying for jobs, 89, 101, 112,
  126–127, 137–138

asking for help, 133–134

asking questions at interviews,
  60–64, 84–87

attire for interviews, 76–77

auditions, 79, 81

B

background networking, 101

bad questions interviewers ask,
  89–90

behavior-description questions,
  61, 79

breaks in employment, 90–91

C

callbacks, waiting for, 12, 27–31,
  47, 49

calls, returning, 29

cards. *See* stickies and cards

career stories, 140

career timelines, 53–57, 93

career transitioning, 147–152

checklist, 159–160

chunking ToDos, 2, 17–18, 20–21,
  31

closed questions, 79

completion rate, 6, 7

contact information, 49

cultural fit, 55, 57–63, 85–87, 89,
  94, 127

current job, explaining why you
  are leaving, 87–88

D

data management, 5, 49, 161

dependent ToDos, 15

Done column (on kanban board),
  12, 25. *See also* kanban boards

dressing for interviews, 76–77

E

education, in résumés, 68

education, pursuing additional,
  130–131

electronic documents, 48–50

electronic project management
  tools, 19, 132

email, 48

emergent projects, 30–31

entry-level experience, 147

etiquette, networking, 104

experimenting with different companies, 137–138

F
facilitated conversations, 39–40
feedback. *See also* reflecting on previous week
importance of, 128–129
from kanban board, 2
opportunities for, 5
qualitative, 36–37
quantitative, 33–36
stickies and, 19, 27
from timeboxes, 8
from unsuccessful interviews, 162
50, workers over, 153–156
first jobs, 54
first week, 12–14, 21–22
Five Whys, 41–43, 124–125, 132
following people on social media, 117–118

G
good enough for now, 24, 31, 32, 46, 121–122, 140–141. *See also* perfectionism
groups, 102–104

H
hashtags, 115–116
help, asking for, 133–134
helping others, 103–104, 133
honesty, 71
humor, 138
hypothetical interview questions, 80

I
ideas, generating, 42, 97, 139, 155
illegal interview questions, 83–84
imposter, felling like, 123

In Progress column (on kanban board), 25. *See also* kanban boards; work in progress (WIP)
incomplete ToDos, 128–129, 160
independent ToDos, 15, 47
indiscriminately applying for jobs, 89, 101, 112, 126–127, 138
informational interviews, 93, 107–108, 162
internships, 147, 151
interview questions, 79–84, 87–91
interviews
appropriate appearance and attire for, 76–77
articulating your career stories, 140
auditions in, 79, 81
feedback from, 45
informational, 93, 107–108, 162
observing during, 78
preparing for, 75–78, 83–84
questions asked by interviewers, 79–84, 87–91
questions to ask at, 60–64, 84–87
thank-you notes following, 91
irrelevant interview questions, 81–83
iteration, 5–6, 45–50

J
job culture, 55, 57–63, 85–87, 89, 94, 127
job descriptions, 129–130, 138
job offers, 93–98, 125–126
job patterns, 53–57, 66. *See also* cultural fit

K
kanban boards. *See also* timeboxes; ToDos

components of, 11–12
creating, 9–12
description of, 2, 7
Parking Lot and, 18, 47, 49, 121, 129
reasons for using, 2–3, 5, 7, 25–27
stickies, using on. *See* stickies and cards
transferring ToDos to, 12–14
using, 21–30

L
lateral positions, 161–162
leading questions, 81
lean and agile principles, 31
line positions, 155–156
LinkedIn. *See also* networking; social media networking
alumni networks, 101–105
building networks, 113–114, 148–149, 151
first-level connections, 103
following people, 118
groups and lists, 102–104
informational interviews and, 107–108
LinkedIn email, 48
for people over 50, 153–154
profile pictures, 24–25, 105–107
profiles, 23–24, 69, 131
recommendations, 151
setting up an account, 22–25, 113
Week One focus on, 13–14
lists, 102–104
living where you have options, 152
loose connections, 104–105, 109–110, 148–149, 151–152
low-volume jobs, 163

M
mailing lists, 103–104
managing yourself, 136–137
marketing messages, 110–111
meta-questions, 79
mind mapping, 43–44
mistakes, dwelling on, 121
multitasking, 6

N
negotiating offers, 96–97
networking
applying focus to, 111–112
background networking, 101
building relationships and, 147–152
early in career, 147–148
etiquette in, 104
with fellow alumni, 101–105
with friends, 151–152
groups and lists for, 102–104
helping others when, 103–104
importance of, 1, 13–14, 45
informational interviews and, 107–108
loose connections in, 104–105, 109–110, 148–149, 151–152
networking support groups, 108
for people over 50, 153–154
at professional meetings, 105, 148–151
targeted, 108–112, 116, 126, 159
using social media, 113–118. *See also* LinkedIn
new grads, 81, 147–148
non-existent jobs, 163
non-paying opportunities, 151

O
objectives in résumés, 67
offers, 93–98, 125–126

older workers, 153–156
one-week timeboxes, 2, 8, 19, 128, 160
online applications, 137–138
open-ended questions, 79
organization, 47–50
organizational culture, 55, 57–63, 85–87, 89, 94, 127

P

Parking Lot, 18, 47, 49, 121, 129
passion, 65
patterns of behavior, 53–57, 66. *See also* cultural fit
Pen column (on kanban board), 12, 27–31, 47, 49. *See also* kanban boards
perfectionism, 18–19, 32, 47, 121–122, 140–141. *See also* good enough for now
personal kanban boards. *See* kanban boards
Plus/Minus/Change (+/-/Δ) review, 37–38
previous job patterns, 53–57, 66. *See also* cultural fit
prioritizing ToDos, 16–17
problem solving, 139
problem-solving skills, interview questions about, 80
procrastination, 2
productivity, 6
professional meetings, 105, 148–151
professionalism, 138
profile pictures, 24–25, 105–107
profiles, LinkedIn, 23–24, 69, 131
project management tools
electronic tools, 19
kanban board. *See* kanban boards

Parking Lot, 18, 47, 49, 121, 129
stickies. *See* stickies and cards
timeboxes. *See* timeboxes
Proud/Oops review, 38–39
pulling work through the system, 7. *See also* kanban boards
purpose, defining your, 64–65

Q

questions, interview, 79–84, 87–91
questions to ask interviewers, 60–64, 84–87

R

ranking ToDos, 16–17
Ready To Do column (on kanban board), 12, 23, 25, 47. *See also* kanban boards
recent graduates, 81, 147–148
recertification, 148
recommendations, 45
recruiters, 141–143
references, 45, 71–73
reflecting on previous week. *See also* feedback
evaluating data, 161
facilitated conversations for, 39–40
Five Whys for, 41–43, 124–125, 132
journaling, 40–41
measuring progress, 33–36
mind mapping for, 43–44
Plus/Minus/Change (+/-/Δ) review, 37–38
Proud/Oops review, 38–39
unfinished ToDos and, 128–129, 160
rejection, 1, 7, 30, 127–128
relationship building, 147–152
relevance, demonstrating, 155

repeating tasks, 5–6, 45–50
résumés
    formats, 67–68
    honesty in, 71
    information to include, 67–70
    iterating, 73–74
    length, 68
    maintaining multiple versions,
        48–49, 74
    publicizing, 45
    redrafting, 135–136
    references and, 71–73
    relying solely on, 127
    spraying, 89, 101, 112, 126–127,
        138
retrospective review. See reflecting
    on previous week
reverse chronological order format,
    67–68
risk management, 8, 42, 132
root cause analysis, 41–43, 124–
    125, 132
Rule of Three, 42, 97, 139, 155

S
scheduling work. See kanban
    boards
searching on Twitter, 114–118
second week, 13–14
self-esteem, 42–43
signboards. See kanban boards
skills, technical, 68, 156
small wins, 139
social media networking, 113–118.
    See also LinkedIn
spray-and-pray, 89, 101, 112, 126–
    127, 138
staff positions, 156
stickies and cards. See also ToDos
    electronic tools vs., 19, 132

moving through kanban board,
    22–28, 47, 116
Parking Lot for, 18, 47, 49, 121,
    129
purpose of, 12, 30, 160
ranking ToDos with, 16–17
strengths/weaknesses, interview
    questions about, 82
success, defining for you, 65–66

T
target lists, 109–110, 111, 112, 116,
    126, 159
targeted marketing plans, 108–
    112
tasks. See ToDos
technical positions, 155–156
technical skills, 68, 156
templates for first week, 12–13
tests, online, 137–138
thank you notes, 91
throughput, 6, 7
timeboxes. See also kanban boards;
    ToDos
    completing small tasks in, 6–7
    description of, 2–3
    limiting weekly ToDos, 17–18
    one-week timeboxes, 2, 8, 19,
        128, 160
    planning, 46–47
    reason for using, 5
ToDos. See also kanban boards;
    timeboxes
    analyzing open, 41–43
    chunking, 2, 17–18, 20–21, 31
    completing one every day, 143
    creating, 12–15
    description of, 9
    focusing on one at a time, 6
    independent, 15, 47

Parking Lot for, 18, 47, 49, 121, 129
ranking, 16–17
size of, 15, 26, 30, 47, 135–136, 143
stickies, using for. *See* stickies and cards
transferring to kanban board, 12–14
unfinished, 128–129, 160
for Week One, 12–14. *See also* Week One
for Week Two, 13–14
working in sequence on, 23–24
tracking data, 5, 49, 161
transferable skills, 163–164
traps and solutions
applying everywhere indiscriminately, 126–127
dependency of team on you, 123–125
education, pursuing additional, 130–131
felling like an imposter, 123
help, not asking for, 133–134
imagining the worst, 131–132
incomplete LinkedIn profiles, 131
job description, not understanding, 129–130, 138
mistakes, dwelling on, 121
offers, written vs. oral, 125–126
perfection, seeking, 18–19, 32, 47, 121–122, 140–141. *See also* good enough for now

rejection, taking it personally, 127–128
relying solely on the perfect résumé, 127
too much work in progress, 128–129. *See also* work in progress (WIP)
truthfulness, 71
Twitter, 114–118. *See also* networking
typecasting, 163–164

U
unfinished ToDos, 128–129, 160

V
visualizing your work, 3, 7, 9–12, 25–27, 128
volunteer work, 151

W
Wednesdays as start of week, 21
Week One, 12–14, 21–22
Week Two, 13–14
work culture, 55, 57–63, 85–87, 89, 94, 127
work habits, 136–137
work in progress (WIP), 6, 42, 46–47, 128–129. *See also* Pen column (on kanban board)
workspaces, 9–10
writing résumés, 67–71, 73–74. *See also* résumés

Z
zombie profiles, 131